The No-Nonsense Approach to Landing a Job

DION YANG

ISBN: 1530465702
ISBN-13: 978-1530465705

DEDICATION

I'd like to give shout-outs to my Mom for being emotionally supportive, my Dad for being tough and putting things into perspective. My best friend Zhen who got me started in the art of the talking the talk, and most importantly myself for taking action and backing up my talk with walking the walk, and everyone who I've come across and talked to in every interview process ever for helping me fine-tune my communication and presentation skills in the pursuit of the no-nonsense approach to landing a job.

CONTENTS

ACKNOWLEDGMENTS

Friends who have been a listening ear and a support structure whenever the career process was going tough.

MILLENNIALS AND THE BIG PICTURE

Most of us have grown up in a world where getting a job, and keeping a job, is no longer a given.

Millennials, the people who are currently the largest workforce in the business world, have seen an economic rise in jobs, it's true. But those facts haven't changed the social narrative that jobs are hard to come by. It's a strange culture of ignoring the steady improvement that is right before our eyes, probably born of years of hardship that made little sense in a modern age.

But there are better statistics to focus on when you head into the job market:

- 63% of the top business executives will be eligible for retirement in the next 5 years, leaving huge gaps in management that will need to be filled.
- In the last 5 years, 89% of new management positions were filled by millennials, rather than baby boomers or any other generation.
- Time magazine reported in 2012 that by 2025, 75% of the global workforce will be filled by millennials.
- Over 63% of millennials have college educations, making us the most educated generation in the current workforce, ever.
- In 2012, 54% of millennials in the workforce had

either already started their own businesses, or were actively working towards doing so.

All these facts add up to one thing: The job openings are there, the ladder is opening up, and the young workforce is booming with people who are stepping in and creating even more jobs.

What does this mean for you?

Hope.

It's a simple word, and it's certainly not the end all, be all of job searching, but if there's anything that studying the current job market should give you, it's a sense of hope for your future. If you've internalized the message that the generation you belong to is lazy, unfocused, and unreliable, let's look at some facts.

Millennials are the most diverse workforce that the United States has ever seen, with over 43% of the generation being made up of non-white individuals. The opportunities for those who may not have found them before are becoming more visible and more present.

This is a generation, and thus a workforce, that is shaped by technology. Progress in the way we utilize technology to improve our lives and our jobs has created one of the most efficient groups in recent history.

After being raised by a generation that was forced into undesirable working habits to pay bills during a recession, millennials are very focused on balance. Social lives, family, hobbies, and creative fulfillment are important to us, and that means that businesses are finding more and more ways to incorporate those factors into their operating procedures.

We now have some of the happiest workplaces in the world, which is leading to more productivity and fewer stress-related health problems.

Over the last three generations, millennials have invested more in human capital than any other. We are learning to pool resources, promote skill training, and mine our colleagues for wisdom and support, eliminating stressful competition and wasteful office politics.

Millennials tend to get married later than their older generation peers, and aren't as likely to purchase houses. This makes them prime employee candidates for start up companies.

Millennials are moving into urban areas much faster than previous generations, and rely less on commuting. In fact, millennials are more likely to focus on jobs that allow them to telecommute, or have flextime, so that they can take advantage of their most productive times.

Overall, this is a generation that is presenting a compelling, valuable workforce. In the coming years, the opportunities for you and your goals will only grow by leaps and bounds. Make your plan, banish the nonsense, and get to work. Your long-term goals are closer than you think.

PART ONE: YOU

It's an unavoidable fact that you'll be searching for a job at least seven to ten times in your adult life. Finding a job – any job – is a migraine ready to be explored, and at the same time how do you find one that's right for you? Next to finding your potential soul mate, choosing the right job, let alone choosing an appropriate career path that fits you, is the most important thing you can do to have a more fulfilled life.

This is a collection of straightforward advice, relevant data, and my own personal experiences that will help you find exactly what you're looking for and tell you how to go about getting there. It's a no-nonsense way of getting a job, for people who want to land a job quickly and who don't enjoy wasting time on not getting responses back on your job applications due to poor presentation, or following job leads that go nowhere, or spending time interviewing with dead-end companies.

In Part One, I'm addressing everything you need to consider about you when it comes to picturing the career track you want to be in and also trying to land a new job.

From the time you're in high school, or maybe even before, you'll hear the question everywhere: What do you want to be when you grow up?

This is a loaded question, because it implies that you

already know everything there is to know about yourself, and what your interests and passions will be for the rest of your life. We're always changing, all the time, so knowing what you "want to be" is always going to change as you grow in your experiences. But there are some better questions you can ask yourself to help answer this one. Like what is your brand?

Your "brand" is basically a fancy business term for how you present yourself to others. It's what makes you stand out; what makes you unique from every other person in the world. Asking yourself how you want others to see you is a big part of understanding what kinds of jobs you might be interested in. Do you want to be seen as honest and reliable? An expert in your field of specialty? Strategic and decisive? Proactive and a team driver? Successful and wealthy? Brilliant and innovative? Kindhearted and entrepreneurial? There are different paths that lead to being seen as someone with each one of these traits.

It's also important to ask yourself who you want to see when you look in the mirror. What's important to your own self-image? If you want to embody the ideals of justice and truth, a career in law enforcement might be your calling, or being batman would be more suited, if you can afford it or get the funding for it, but realistically, it's all about understanding what your "brand" is, and then understanding how to find the right audience for that brand.

The second part to figuring out an ideal career path is by assessing your needs. What do you need in order to have a happy, healthy life? What's going to make you feel fulfilled?

If your needs are simply to pay the bills and enjoy a beer on the weekends, then a 9 to 5 that pays well and doesn't tend to send work home with you is a valid choice. If you need to travel to be happy, then maybe a job that takes you out of the country is a better choice.

Above the simplest survival needs is the need to feel safe. For you, that may mean living in a specific region or neighborhood, or it may relate to job security.

The next need is the need to belong. Feeling like you have a purpose in your company, and that your work benefits the greater picture, makes it easier to justify doing tasks and working long hours that you may not want to.

The next need is esteem, which ties in with belonging. We as people need to feel like we are respected, and like our contributions not only benefit the big picture, but are valued.

The final need is self-actualization, which means that a person needs to feel that they are utilizing their highest potential. It's this need that drives us to push for promotions, to seek out careers that are high-stress, and to feel unfulfilled doing menial tasks every day.

When you are considering what job will help you realize this need, keep in mind that you've got to fulfill the primary needs (paying the bills, feeing safe, having a valued purpose) first, but keep in mind that the ultimate goal is a career that makes you feel like you're reaching the pinnacle of who and what you can be.

Choosing your career path really isn't that difficult when you know yourself and trust your gut. But when you are still starting out or you've haven't had experience trying different fields, jobs or experiencing different companies, you will need some guidance to push you into a direction for exploration. Let's look at how to go about exploring finding that job, and some tips for presenting yourself as the best possible candidate.

1. THE SEARCH BEGINS

Am I in the Right City?

Finding a job in the field and/or industry that you want to work in depends on three things: location, location, and location.

Where you live is as critical to your job hunt as what you do. The market for jobs in your area depends on a lot of factors, and working in your chosen field may mean that you're going to have to move if you want to remain relevant, consistently be challenged, and stay sharp.

Demographics

The demographics of your area affect what kinds of businesses and manufacturers will move to the area. A business' first goal is to be where their ideal client base is. If you want to work in high-end fashion, for example, living in an area that is populated by wealthy women is far more likely to result in a larger amount of job opportunities than living in a rural area populated by working-class families.

This factor also affects how much money you can expect to make in your job. City demographics and sites like http://www.glassdoor.com report on the average income of people in relevant positions for companies in specific areas, which is how businesses decide what the base pay should be for a position. You will find it easier to earn six figures if you live in a competitive area where the top companies are opening doors.

If you live in an area filled with elderly retirees and almost zero competition in terms of industry and young professionals, then you will find that the average income is going to be considerably lower. However, the cost of living will be lower as a result, so it's a trade-off worth considering.

Relevance

Career choices in a specific city also depend on staying relevant to the geography and cultural climate of the area. If you live in the tropics, you're unlikely to find a job working a ski lift, just like someone living in the far north probably won't be able to start their own organic pineapple farm.

In addition, the ethics and interests of the area's population factor into what types of businesses you'll find there.

In a large sized city with people who might have more liberal values, you might find it easier to relate to people within the company if you are from a similar upbringing and background. They will also have an easier time relating to you because of the cultural diversity present in such areas.

For example, I grew up in New York City and was used to city life and diverse cultures. Being direct with my ideas and opinions was just a part of life. When I moved to the Bay Area in northern California, I worked in many different companies in the cities that were considered more suburban, and not as culturally diverse, or as exposed to the harsh realities of life with the exclusion of gangs or homelessness out in the open. Everything in these cities are spread so far apart from each other that you have to drive everywhere. This plays a big part of how people behave in general because in a big city typically people walk and talk public transportation and this creates a different atmosphere of people who can't afford to be lazy in their attitudes because they won't survive otherwise.

In every company that I worked at there, I noticed that the workplaces were not as diverse and that the values were considerably different from what I was used to. Because of that, I never felt like I fit into those companies, even though I tried to adapt to their cultures. I felt that I was being disingenuous to myself and didn't want to compromise myself to fit into a place that lacked the values that I strongly believed in.

In contrast, I'm sure that people from smaller towns might be shocked when they go to work in a larger city. It may be incredibly different from how they grew up, and they might find city life too much to handle.

Comparing to Similar Cities

When you're considering the next step in your career, moving to a new city or town might become unavoidable. Particularly if you live in a rural area, there simply may be no opportunities for you to go after to get the career of your dreams. Moving is a big decision, and one that can be a problem if you live in your city because of family or because you love that area.

One of the things you can do to make that decision easier is to look for similar cities that have better job markets for your industry. Things you'll probably want to consider include:

- The cultural climate: Is it similar to the climate of your current home? This includes more than just the weather. Do the people who live in this area share your basic values? If you care deeply about being exposed to diverse view-points, you'll want to find a city that has a population that reflects that. If it's animal welfare or being surrounded by those of a similar religious faith that you look for, those are things that can be judged based on what types of organizations are in the area.

• Educational options: If you have a family, or plan to, the schools you'll send your kids to plays an important part in where you live, but what about you? Do you plan on going back to school, or do you want to have the option nearby?

• Average income: These statistics can be found on websites like http://www.city-data.com, or from http://factfinder.census.gov. If you want to make a certain salary, then obviously you need to find the areas where the average salary is higher for your given industry because that area is ripe for that industry and because competing companies are opening shop in that area to get a piece of that money as well.

• Cost of living: Can you afford to live in this new city now, and on what you plan to negotiate for when applying for jobs? One good way to get an understanding of the cost of living in a city is to look at the cost of homes and apartments. Websites like Craigslist, Trulia, Zillow, and Apartments.com will give you an idea of what most people in the area expect to pay in rent or mortgage. Also factor in driving or general commuting times if you plan on living slightly farther away in order to try to find cheaper living costs. For me personally the mental costs and spending hours in traffic cannot be justified by saving a few hundred dollars per month. But a fair compromise would be if the city has a decent public transit system that can get you to work in a reasonable amount of time while sidestepping the need to drive yourself.

- The population of the area based on age: You can tell a lot about the future of a city's industrial development based on the largest age group in the population.
- An area with a largely young population is usually ripe with opportunities to find work with tech companies, start-ups, and entertainment companies.
- Alternatively, if you're looking for a career in the healthcare field, an area populated by middle-aged or elderly citizens is likely to have more work opportunities.

Look around for where your industry is booming to find good options when considering a move.

Where Do I Look?

Once you've decided what city you want to focus your search, the next question you'll be asking is where to look for a job within that city.

When you're searching for jobs in a specific career, there are multiple ways to discover currently open opportunities on the market at any given time. Either through the time-honored tradition of networking, through recruiters, through job aggregation sites, directly on a given company's website, through social media or through alumni resources through your school.

Networking

Networking is a time-honored way of landing a job. Knowing the right person can open the door to an internship, entry-level job or other mid-level to senior level position that may not have been easily accessible if you came in through regular means with no contacts at a given company.

As social creatures, we're all more likely to take the word of people we trust over hiring some random person off the street — that's just how the game of networking works. We prefer to trust the opinion that we feel is the least risky. It's the same for people who will be interviewing and, ultimately having a hand in the decision to hire you. If you can give them the word of a trusted colleague that you are a low-risk choice, you're more likely to get the job.

People that you can turn to when networking include old work colleagues, college classmates or professors, and ironically all of these people can be found on LinkedIn and are hopefully somewhat connected in one way or another and you should also be a point of making connections as well so that you can build up a network of people who will think of you in the future. Another popular method is to attend networking events, where people specifically get together to talk and make connections, but typically you will find people looking to hire for freelance work more than people who can pass on your resume to their managers.

Here are some tips for making an impression when you're around the right people at networking events:

- Listen more than you speak, and ask questions to keep them talking. It can be tempting to try to sell yourself when you're trying to make a contact, but people are more likely to remember someone who made them feel good about themselves.

- Make sure your business card stands out. These people probably have a stack of boring, white cards that they toss out after every networking event. Find a way to make yours special.
- Find a way to arrange a second meeting. Just like being on a first date, the goal of the initial networking meeting is to get to that second one. People are far more likely to remember someone they've met more than once. If you know the person you're speaking to will be at another event, tell them you'll see them there, and then follow up on that.

Recruiters

Recruiters can be a job-seeker's dream or nightmare. Their job is to bring the opportunity to you, so you don't have to run around chasing leads.

Recruiters can be found at job fairs or any event where there are people looking for work, but you will most likely stumble across them when applying to jobs online, through LinkedIn, or when you add your resume to a job-posting aggregation site. When talking to a recruiter, you'll want to keep two things in mind:

First, not all recruiters are created equal. Some recruiters usually send tons of resumes to companies in batches, just trying to meet their fee quota for the month, and if they don't have a good relationship with the company, you are just another name in a stack of them. In those cases, you are only as good as you sound on paper. Other recruiters try to find and screen the quality candidates and then pitch those candidates to a few companies that they have working relationships with. These recruiters can usually get you in to bigger companies if you have what they are looking for in terms of skill sets and or experience.

Second, they are working for the company, not for you. A recruiter can sometimes be a powerful network contact to have in your corner, especially if you are new to the area, so it's best to not be rude to the ones who have proven that they can land you multiple phone screens. If they are a good recruiter, then the chances are that they have the ability to get your resume directly to the hiring manager's inbox.

Typically, the bigger recruiting agencies have their own offices and work high volume and do a baseline level of screening in order to maintain their business. So some of the things that you may encounter is that you might not be able to get a pay rate that you want because they are low-balling both you and their client to get the work. Another thing would be some of the projects that they have to offer may have short durations from 2 weeks to 3 months. So it's best to think about if you want to spend time jumping from client to client with potential gaps in your employment, earning less than what you would need to cover your living expenses.

So just keep a few of these things in mind when you are talking to recruiters over the phone or in-person. Do you want to be dicked around or can you put your foot down and not let yourself be abused by these practices?

Job Aggregation Sites

A job aggregator website gathers job postings from around the Internet, not only from public posting sites, but also from private company boards and specific career sites.

These types of search engines give you the best shot at finding opportunities because they cut down on the amount of sites you have to go through to find individual job leads. Rather than have to go to 20 sites, you can limit it to a handful to find leads.

Some of the most popular job aggregation sites include:

- http://www.indeed.com
- http://www.simplyhired.com
- http://www.linkedin.com/job/
- http://www.glassdoor.com
- http://www.monster.com

One of the drawbacks is that sometimes you can't apply for a job on their mobile website, which is something that I like to do when I'm out and about and don't have my laptop computer with me. So what I do is email myself a list of postings that I couldn't apply for online and apply to them when I get home. It's annoying but at least I get the searching part done on the go and keep things moving forward.

Direct Company Sites

Finally, if you already have a few companies in mind that you want to work for, searching their website for career options should be your first step.

Usually these can be found under "Careers" or "Work for Us" sections, but if you can't find those, searching the site for the keywords "career" or "job" should lead you to the right page. You'll be able to see any current positions that are open to the public, and this is often the best way to get specific job requirements straight from the horse's mouth.

The company's size is related to how often you'll get a reply when you contact them through this avenue. The smaller the company, the more likely you are to get quick responses. Likewise, larger companies can take a while, or not even reply at all, so you may have to follow up with them.

Social Media

It doesn't seem like the best place to search for professional connections, but social media is often a place to get the most up-to-date job postings, and to make contacts.

Most companies, big and small, a have social media presence now, and if they don't, their managers and employees probably do. Getting involved in the social media circles of professionals in your field can help you create the network you need. All it takes is one comment from someone's Twitter account that a local company is expanding their business, and you now have a lead to follow.

You can also establish yourself as an up-and-coming face in the field. If you aren't very well educated or skilled in the field, you should tread lightly here; but if you do already possess niche skills and experience, you can use social media as a sort of living resume for potential references and employers.

Get involved with the discussions that surround your field, post about current events in the field, and present yourself as a competent professional. It may be that you impress the right person at the right time.

Alumni Resources

Just because you aren't in college anymore doesn't mean you are cut off from the resources you once enjoyed. In fact, alumni often have their own networking sites and message boards set up.

Get in touch with your old university and find out what services they offer; you may even be able to get help from a career coach or mentor as you go about searching for a job.

But one of the biggest things to keep in mind is that some of these departments can be understaffed and the leads they might have are usually going to be entry-level positions that may or may not be beneficial towards getting your foot in the door experience.

Law of Spamming Until Something Sticks

The "Law of Spamming until Something Sticks" has been my process for the longest time, ever since I started looking for my first job. It's the only way to move forward without wasting massive amounts of time doing nothing.

The bottom line is that the more you apply to the jobs that seem like they are a fit, the more responses you will get in a shorter amount of time.

Every job interview with a new company is a fresh experience. Just because you've been turned down the last four times doesn't mean you should count on a negative response on the fifth. Every company is looking for something different in a new team member, so there is no correlation between this one and the last. The attitude you should take here is to follow the "Law of Spamming until Something Sticks".

You are going to have to send out mass amounts of emails, you are going to have to make follow-up calls or emails over and over, and you're going to have to register and submit resumes with at least 30-40 job application websites every month. That translates to at least 10 per week, which in my opinion, still might be on the light side depending on where you live.

It's a frustrating process sometimes. I once tried to upload my resume to a website after filling out a ton of questions, only to find that the upload button didn't work in Google

Chrome. My anger was only barely contained as I had to switch to Firefox to finish the application, but I had a concrete process to follow and I had to meet my quota for the week so I hammered-on and completed the application.

This process has been time tested by me and a few other friends and acquaintances that I have coached, and the ultimate goal is to get your phone ringing so you can move on to the next step in the process. But before we can start, we need to figure out what we are ultimately looking for in our next job.

What Am I Ultimately Looking For?

When considering your next job, there are four types of business environments that all have different cultures, working styles, ethics policies and practices, and pay rates.

When you are first starting out, you probably won't have any idea what to expect from each of these environments, but as you go on and gain more infield experience, you'll learn which is best suited to you. Still, it's a good idea to do some research and read other peoples stories about each type of work environments so you can make an informed guess about which you'd prefer to work with.

Big Corporation

The Big Corporation is the most varied working climate out there. Every single large corporation has a totally different mindset and feel, and that's largely due to the people working there.

Everything stems directly from the hiring manager. If the hiring manager takes care to choose people who work well together, are generally pleasant to be around, and potentially share some similar working values, then you'll probably find that you really enjoy working there. But if the hiring manager doesn't take these things into consideration, a big corporation can feel like a prison with each co-worker being part of their own clique that won't let you in because of personality incompatibility, so you start your own clique and then you have clique wars where everyone refuses to ask each other for help.

When I apply for a position at one of these companies, I always look for a hiring manager I can get along with first. Chances are if I like them, I'll probably get along with the rest of the team.

The second thing I look for is a team that is filled with people I can see myself working around long term. If they aren't team players or just aren't nice people to be around, it'll be a lot harder to enjoy your time with that company.

Large corporations have the most opportunity of all for moving up, and doing so quickly. You're also more likely to build your network with people who have true influence in the entire industry. With more money and more employees, these companies are sometimes likely to be the ones following the most innovative new ideas in your industry.

But, that's not always true across the board, of course. They may be so far behind current processes and technologies that you just wonder how they can still make money, when their internal workings are far from stellar. So if that's something that's important to you, you will need to investigate the company's innovations, technologies and processes if you can.

Past the Startup Phase Company

A medium to small sized company that is past the startup phase can be a hard environment to nail down. You're more likely to get to know mostly everyone in the company and you're probably more likely to get to know those people on a more personal level. Often these companies have less behind-the-scenes politics.

Climbing the ladder in these companies can be tricky. While the growth is obviously there, since they've moved on from startup stage, a small company is still going to have tight budgets in place. It may be a situation where hiring and promotions are scarce, or promotions are going to employees who've been there longest or it may go to people who've demonstrated leadership skills and accountability.

These companies are in a unique position in their industries. With less money and less employees, they can't always be the industry leaders that a large corporation can. They may not have access to the best equipment or data.

But because they aren't in the public eye or under the scrutiny of a board of directors, these companies are more likely to be able to take risks and follow new lines of thought. If you want to work in a business setting where you still have some opportunity to think outside the box, this may be your best bet.

Startup

A startup company has a lot of cons if you aren't ready to commit large amounts of your waking hours and weekends to work, but the pros can be very tempting. Let's start with the "hours" conversation.

If you've ever wondered what it would be like to spend 14 hours a day away from your home and have next to no social life, then the startup life is perfect for you. It's true that startups require a big commitment from their employees if they want to succeed. When you're just starting out, it takes every single second of productivity you can squeeze out of a day to move up in the ranks.

You're also probably not what a startup is looking for unless you have a very narrow, specific set of skills. Startups rely on people who are masters at one particular system or procedure, because again, they need someone who can perform at top productivity levels right out of the gate. Unless you happen to be an expert in a very specific niche skill set, you may find it hard to get hired with a startup.

There's also the risk that your job may not be there next year, next month, or even next week. As startups develop, jobs get merged or split or shuffled around until everyone learns what works best for the company. Systems get replaced with something that works better, meaning your narrow skill set no longer applies and you'll need to adapt to stay current or be left behind struggling.

There are some major upsides to working for a startup, though. The most obvious being that climbing the ladder is basically a given. If you get in when there are only a handful of employees, you'll be one of the first names to come up for promotion.

You'll also be able to gain valuable experience far more quickly than any other type of company, in more than just your area of expertise. Startups require a lot of employees to do the work of three or four different positions, so you'll have an impressive resume when you've finished your stay and are ready to move on to a different company.

Getting Your Foot in the Door

When you are first starting to build your resume, my advice would be to take any entry-level position in your career field, regardless of the type of company it is.

Chances are, you won't stay in the same company you start with for the rest of your career, and those foot-in-the-door positions add to your experience. They can help you get those networking contacts we talked about before. This is also the only way you'll really start to understand the differences between company types first hand, so that you can later go after the one you really want to land a position in.

Your Portfolio

Many different kinds of careers require a portfolio, which can be as important, or even more so, than your resume.

If you don't have the most impressive list of previous employers, but your portfolio blows the hiring manager away, you're probably more likely to get hired than someone with a lackluster portfolio but an impressive resume. In this one area, results and skills give you an edge over experience.

Visual Trades

For artists and graphic designers, the importance of a portfolio is a no-brainer. You have to show that your work is not only of high quality, but also in line with what the company wants.

You also need to be able to communicate through your visual work, especially if you're going to be creating advertisements, mockups, prototypes and things of the sort. Companies probably also want to know if you have a mastery of more than one style, proving that you're valuable for more than just one type of project.

Engineering Trades

Architects, engineers, and urban planners are going to

have to show that they can effectively design structures that can be built.

If you have no experience having your designs translated into real structures, your portfolio needs to be even more impressive. You've got to show projected materials, costs, why you chose the materials and tools that you did, and any other considerations that came up in your design projects.

Software and Programming Trades

For computer software and programming engineers, your portfolio will need to show that you are capable of not only designing effective software, but also that you can fix problems, think of unorthodox solutions, collaborate on projects, and think about scalability as well as maintainability. If you haven't worked on a successful software launch yet, the portfolio is the place to show that you've got the chops for the job.

Writing and Editing Trades

Writing and editing samples are vital for getting hired with a newspaper, journal, or professional blog. Particularly for writers who haven't been published, samples are the only way an employer will be able to judge your ability. An editor may need to include before-and-after projects that show how their eagle eye improved a published piece.

Research and Development Trades

If your career field is in research or academia, then you'll probably need a portfolio of published papers, or at least the dissertations and other similar papers you wrote in school. You may also need the logs you kept while you did research projects to show your ability to follow procedures and draw conclusions.

Speakers and Educating Trades

Motivational speakers or educators might need to include transcripts or even video of themselves as examples of their work in a portfolio.

No one wants to hire a speaker and then discover that they just don't have stage personality. It might also be a good idea to include statistics that show how your class or discussion topics changed or improved the performances and behaviors of those who attended.

With all of these portfolio types, you should take care to mention in detail any collaboration you've worked on. You may want to include performance reviews that mentioned your teamwork abilities, or a detailed breakdown of how each person on the team contributed to the project.

Collaboration

Companies always want to know if you are a team player. It's rare in today's business world that you will be working alone; since a lot of companies have a tendency to over-promise results to their clients and overbook work all of the time.

You may be collaborating with people who have less technical skills than you, or more specialized knowledge in other areas. Companies want to know that you have experience working with others, and if you don't, you should be prepared with specific answers to the potential questions about how you would have done a project differently had you been collaborating.

Making a Plan

Searching for a job can be a daunting task when you're just starting. It might seem like you're stumbling over the decisions, barely even sure of what you do want. As you are considering all the information that you find on potential companies and cities, you also need to sit down with your own goals and solidify what you want.

Making goals for your career actually involves two different sets of goals, with many steps in-between. Before we get into that, let's talk about something that you need to keep in mind whenever you write down any goal, no matter where you are in the process.

SMART Criteria (Setting Goals)

The idea of the SMART criteria, in the context of personal development, is to define a set of principles to aid in the setting of goals, more specifically, the letters in SMART break down into helping to write out goals and objectives which are:

- Specific
- Measurable
- Attainable
- Relevant
- Time Bound

When you make your goals, make sure that each one, no matter how small, fits each one of these descriptions.

Is it specific? Don't simply write: "Get a new job", write: "Get hired at a social media tech company or a company that is closely related with social media technology within their marketing department and do work that is closely related to social media marketing".

Is it measurable? If your goal is to be happier with your own performance, how are you going to know that you've achieved it? Happiness isn't something that can be scientifically measured. Instead use something that you can chart that relates, such as "Get hired at a company where the team and the management is passionate about quality over quantity and are passionate about contributing excellent work."

Is your goal attainable? It should be something that you can achieve in the time given. Don't set yourself up for failure by aiming for getting hired at a company and earning half a million dollars if the industry that you work in doesn't even pay close to that amount, instead do research and figure out what the expected salaries are for your current experience level and work towards that amount, and if you achieve that goal before the year is up, you can press yourself to figure out how to exceed it.

Is it relevant? Make sure that your small goals are truly helping you achieve your main goal. If your big yearly goal is to move to a new city for new job opportunities, consider what smaller goals you can aim for to help you get closer to that move.

Finally, is *it time bound?* An open-ended goal rarely hits it's mark. If you don't give yourself a deadline, you won't feel the sense of urgency and you'll procrastinate and probably get comfortable in your current place.

Here's an example of a SMART goal I would write:

Specific: I want to move to San Francisco, California in order to be able to take advantage of all the exciting technology companies that are out there, and get more experience with current trends and methodologies in software development.

Measurable: Need to make list of what it would cost to move to San Francisco and what the living costs are and if I need to split the rent with roommates and what areas are decent areas to live in and what companies I'm interested in working at.

Attainable: Yes. It's doable if I either have the savings on hand or land a job first and potentially get a relocation stipend from the new job.

Relevant: It's relevant to helping me move to where the technology sector is growing and booming.

Time Bound: I plan to figure out the living costs within 2 weeks and start looking for a job there immediately and plan to land a job within 6 months.

Long Term Goals

Long-term goals are more loosely defined than short-term goals. These goals are "big ideas", missions, visions, or a state of being that you want to reach.

- You want to "be successful" in your field
- You want to "live comfortably" on your salary
- You want to "help others"

These are examples of long-term goals that you want to achieve through your career.

How do you decide what your long-term goal is?

First you need to look at your current life. Analyze your

lifestyle now. Ask yourself what you do or do not like about who you are, or how you live. Look at the things you are passionate about, and think about your strengths and weaknesses. What sorts of motivations or activities always seem to pop back up in your life no matter where you are?

Next, you need to define what success means to you. It's something different for everyone. For some, success might mean having zero debt, a garage full of cars, and a mansion. For others, success could be sending their kids to the best schools and paying for their parents' retirement. Whatever success looks like for you, write it down.

Now, using the information you just gathered about yourself, identify the highest positions in your industry that match up with your ideas about success, your strengths and weaknesses, and the lifestyle you want to have. That position may not exist. Maybe you need to create it.

Once you've identified the positions that give you the best shot at meeting your own success head on, you'll have your long-term goal in place. Next come the short-term goals.

Short-Term Goals

Short-term goals should be thought of as plateaus. As you climb the mountain towards your long-term goal, these are places where you can measure your progress and gather more supplies for the next climb. You'll be able to look back down at where you've been, and reassess your plan for continuing upward, at each of these stops.

After you've done your research to find the highest positions that will lead to the life you want, now you need to list the necessary qualifications and experience that it will take to get to those positions.

This is going to take some research. Figure out the paths that lead from entry-level grunt to bigwig guru, and write it down step by step. Sometimes this information can be found by studying the company. If they list their employees on their website, you should see a clear path that leads from Assistant, Team Associate, Manager, and on up the ranks.

If you haven't chosen a particular company to focus on, then you'll need to look into the way your chosen field is usually broken down. For example, if you work in the medical field, your job may start as an Aide, then move on to a Medical Assistant, before finally landing on Licensed Practitioner. This is an easy path to follow because it depends on the level of education you have.

If you work in a field that relies more on experience rather than higher education, go to job aggregation sites, and try to find listings within your field for entry level applicants, applicants with 3 to 5 years of experience, and applicants with higher levels of experience. List the job openings you find sorted by the required experience level. That will help you lay out a map of how employees usually work their way up in your field.

After that? You just need to make a plan to move up in these ranks. If you'll need more education to move up to a higher position, you'll need to potentially look into more schooling. If you'll be relying on experience and excellent work to move up in your company, you'll now know which positions you're aiming for, and can tailor your approach to improve your chances of promotion. For example:

If step one is "get hired with Big Company A", then you need to get hired with Big Company A. You've picked up this book, so you've already started your journey on honing in your goals and lining up your beliefs and values with the job that you want.

If step two is "Get promoted to Team Leader", you'll need to consider how you're going to convince your managers to promote you after some time there. Do you need to take some courses in leadership? Do you need to improve your technical career-related skills? Remember to utilize the SMART criteria for each of these steps.

Write your goals down, and keep them visible. Keeping your plans where you can see them and reflect on them can keep you going through the tough times and keep you focused on your goals. Visualization methods have been proven to help you feel more motivated, so if you ever do get stuck, you can look back on your goals and spend a few minutes considering how great it's going to feel when you do reach the goal that you set out to complete.

You may even want to make a spreadsheet or keep a log of each small step you overcome, so that you can track and see how far you've come in reaching your goal. In fact, noting any challenges or unexpected twists you faced at each step can help you become more prepared for the next step on your journey to your long term goals.

Now that you have a plan in place, you're on track to fulfilling the milestones on the road towards reaching that long-term goal.

2. PRESENTATION

Remember when we were talking about personal branding in part one of this book? Getting others to perceive you in the way that you want them to largely comes down to how you present yourself.

Once you've decided where and how you're applying, presentation is everything, and it starts long before you ever talk to someone. Presentation has multiple steps, and preparing for each one is the only way to be sure that you're going to communicate exactly who you are and why you're the best candidate for the job.

How Do You Come Off?

We all like to say that we wouldn't judge a book by its cover, but that's untrue. People make judgments based on their first impressions every day. It's part of our evolutionary instincts, to quickly scan and assess new people, places, and things for potential danger or use. So, the first impression you give is critical.

Understanding how you come off isn't exactly the easiest thing to explain. It's about your general attitude. How your posture, handshake, eye contact, and things like that communicate your likability are part of it, but it's also in the way you answer questions.

When an interviewer talks to you, how you speak is just as important as what you say. They'll be able to tell how you feel about the company, how you see yourself, and how well you'll be able to fit in with the team and company, just based on this impression.

If you like the company, and you want to be working there, you should take great pains to come across as the most qualified candidate they have. You need to be open to their questions, even the tough ones, and your general attitude should be one of wanting to work with them for both their benefit and your own.

A Confident Attitude

Being confident and being cocky are two different things. When you're speaking to a hiring manager, you need to make them feel as through you are rock solid in your abilities and your problem solving skills.

There is a science behind body language and communication that you can hack to achieve the effect you want. Even if you don't feel it, practicing these easy tricks will convince anyone that you are the most confident person in the room.

Posture and Body Language

When you think about how you're going to act in an interview, at a networking event, or at a meeting with a recruiter, you probably think about the words you're going to say more than anything. But the way you carry yourself and utilize your body goes a very long way to making people feel like they can trust you.

Posture is one of the easiest things to fix. Whether you are sitting or standing, your basic posture should focus on three things: back straight, shoulders down, chin up.

When your back is straight and your shoulders are down and back, you appear comfortable and in control of your body. Keeping your chin up establishes that you are not stressed out, because lowering your chin is a nervous habit that animals use to protect their vulnerable necks.

When you are seated, you should find the right balance between slouching back, and leaning forward. One is too casual, and the other can come across as either too forceful, or very nervous.

Try this instead: sit so that when you stand, you do not have to lean forward in order to stand back up. From sitting, you should be able to smoothly stand right back up using only your legs. This means you'll need some room between your knees or calves, and the edge of the chair. Sitting like this forces you to sit straight, but you're also focused on not leaning forward.

Body language can be harder to fix, because a lot of it is unconscious. Below are some important body language tips.

Your handshake is often one of the first ways a manager, recruiter, or possible contact will get an impression of you. Keep your handshake firm, but don't break their hand. It's not a contest, but nothing is worse than a dead fish handshake.

When you are standing, remember that you can and should take up space. Even if you are in a crowded area, you have a right to be there. Don't pull your body close or hunch in an attempt to "be polite". Stand normally, with strong posture, and wide shoulders. You don't have to spread out and make others uncomfortable, but you also want to make sure that the right people see you.

When you are standing, make sure that your weight is evenly distributed on both of your feet, and don't fidget back and forth. Shifting your weight, or keeping it all on one side, is a primitive signal that you are preparing to run. It shows that you are not confident, and are looking for a quick exit. Additionally, you should take deep breaths through your stomach in order to calm your nerves and keep your voice supported.

Keep about 80% eye contact when they are speaking and when you are speaking. Keep it friendly, but direct. Looking to either side when speaking can indicate lying or nervousness. If direct eye contact all the time feels too aggressive, there are a few tricks that come in handy:

First, try to focus on a part of their face that is roughly eye level, such as their nose or forehead. They won't be able to tell that you aren't looking them directly in the eye, and you'll feel more comfortable.

Second, find something that is at eye level on the wall behind them. Any time you feel yourself losing eye contact, direct your gaze to that object or focal point. That will stop you from dropping your gaze, and appearing dishonest.

In general, keep your body still. Don't fidget once you've been seated. Keep your legs still, don't shift your weight around, and avoid touching your face or hair. All of these motions make you look nervous and inexperienced. A confident person does not need to waste energy on needless motion, but also you don't want to stifle yourself so much that you start to feel like a stiff robot.

Your hands are a big indicator of how you feel in a situation. Above all, your hands should stay visible and relaxed. Hiding your hands is often seen as a sign that you have something to hide. Keep your hands out of your pockets, and don't cross your arms. That posture signifies that you are closed off. When speaking, keep your hands still, or jot down the answers that they give to your questions on a notepad if you need something to keep them busy.

Using hand gestures when you speak can work, if you're emphasizing your points, but be careful not to over do it, or use gestures that are too large. That can look chaotic, and like you're trying to distract an interviewer from a weakness in your presentation.

When you're walking, move at a steady pace that is neither too slow, nor too fast. Moving too quickly, especially, can make you seem like you would rather be anywhere but there.

So all in all, just keep an eye out for the most common problems listed above, and practice using better body language with your friends and family and in general to get comfortable with how it feels to utilize more comfortable body language.

Speaking and Mental Tricks

Body language and your verbal communication skills go hand-in-hand to make you appear confident and in control.

Just like you should walk at a steady pace, my number one tip for speaking like a professional is to slow down. Most people speak way faster than they need to in a presentation or when talking about themselves. You have to remember that the people listening need time to not only hear you, but also to process and analyze what you are saying. Slow down, and allow for natural pauses in your speech.

When considering how you sound, there are two things

that will give you an authoritative tone: lower your voice, and don't end your sentences as if you are asking a question.

Using a lower pitch when speaking makes people feel like you know what you're talking about; that's why so many news anchors have deep voices. Even female news reporters tend to use a lower pitch when speaking.

Ending your sentences on a firm period, rather than a question mark, is a no-brainer, but many younger people do this almost out of habit now. Pay attention to the way your voice rises and falls at the end of your sentences. It should stay firm, rather than rising in either pitch or speed.

When speaking to someone whose judgment could be essential for your progress, there are three words you should always avoid: usually, confused, might and likely.

Usually is a weak word that leaves too much open to question. If you say "I usually work best in a small team", you sound like you haven't had enough experience to be absolutely sure of your strengths. Instead, just say "I work best in small teams", and leave it at that. You know yourself, and they need to know that you can identify and work with your strengths.

Confused is a word that might slip out when you are asking questions of a manager or a recruiter. On the surface, it doesn't sound so bad to say "I'm confused about the hiring timeline, could you go over it again?" However, this word places the problem on your ability to understand things, rather than on the clarity of the topic. You never want to appear as though you can't get a good grasp on a clearly presented idea.

Instead, just ask them to clarify the subject, or ask specific questions to get the clarification you need. In the example above, you'd say instead: "Will you clarify a point about the hiring timeline? How many business days do you allow before you begin calling for interviews?"

The last two words is might and likely. In context, they mean the same thing. If a person of influence asks you what your plans are after you get hired, or if you don't get hired, you should never say something like: "I might go back to school", or "I'll likely start working towards a promotion within my first year." These words make you appear as though you don't have a firm plan in place. Employers especially want to know that you know how to set goals and go after them.

Just get rid of these words and say honestly what you'll be doing. "If I don't get the opportunity to work in this position, I will be going back to school." That's easy, and you sound much more confident about your direction.

One common mistake that a lot of new job seekers make is to attempt to qualify themselves when they are introduced. They'll say, "Hello, I'm Tiffany Brown, and I was referred to your company by..." or, "Hello, I'm Aaron Smith, and I worked on a project last year with..." At your first introduction, just greet them and say your name. That's it. "Hello, I am (name)." This does two things.

First, it makes you sound like you are confident in your reasons for being there. If the person you're speaking to doesn't know why you are there, they'll either ask, or they'll do what a lot of people do, and hide their ignorance by playing along until they do understand.

Second, it immediately opens up a dialogue. The next thing that the other person will do is greet you back, and then ask about you, or why you're here. It gets you both talking, which leads to more conversation.

All of these things can become second nature with practice. If you are an exceptionally shy person, or you don't have much practice with speaking to people in a formal setting, there are two more tricks that you can keep up your sleeve to help get over those feelings of nervousness.

Chew gum right before you walk in, or as you are waiting. Our brains have evolved to constantly be on the lookout for danger. It's the instinct that has kept us alive and thriving for centuries. One thing about animals who watch for danger: they don't eat when they are afraid. Eating makes you stop, takes your eyes away from watching, and can overpower your other senses.

So, when you eat, you are sending a signal to your brain that all is clear. Your brain assumes that you have assessed the threat level, and found a safe place to eat. The motion of chewing makes your brain release anxiety-calming chemicals. Just be sure that you get rid of the gum before you speak.

If you are at a networking event, or a company event, trying to make new contacts, the best thing to do is give yourself a very short time limit to approach people. For example, if you see someone that you know you want to speak to, give yourself only five seconds to approach them. If you hesitate for any longer, that person is off-limits, and you've just lost a great potential contact. That small window forces you into action.

Being confident should never come across as fake, but as you practice and use these tips, you'll develop a natural routine that will help you take control of any situation.

How Does Your Resume Look?

Think of your resume as your wingman for this interview. It's the friend that's going to keep popping into the conversation with interesting, relevant points about you that make you seem like a better candidate each time the hiring manager refers to it.

Or at least, it should. If you have a strong resume, this is exactly what will happen. The manager will find plenty of points to discuss with you, meaning that you'll be given the time to go into plenty of detail explaining how you'll be the best fit for the company. The longer your interview lasts, the more time you have to shape that first impression into something favorable.

On the other hand, if your resume is weak, and you somehow still made it into an interview, you're both going to be grasping for anything to discuss. Even if your first impression is a good one, people are more likely to recall candidates that they spent more time with when it comes time to narrow the field. So how do you make your resume strong?

The key is to be detailed where it's relevant. For every job, internship, study program, or volunteer position you've had that relates in any way to what you'll be doing at that company, you need to list, in detail, these things:

- Your specific duties
- The tools you worked with
- The collaboration involved with your position
- Any social or extracurricular activities that were a part of the position
- Extra duties you performed that weren't in your job description
- Education you received in the position

Anything that gives the hiring manager something to ask you about means more time in their office, which translates to a better and stronger impression.

The style of your resume should reflect the job you want. While all resumes need to be free of errors and written in a clear and readable language, free of slang; an editor's resume, for example, should most definitely be perfect. Likewise, a graphic designer's resume might draw on their design skills to create a document that stands out a little with unique elements.

If you're unsure how your resume should physically look, the standard rule of thumb is to err on the side of professionalism. A readable resume with plenty of detail is more important than a uniquely designed document.

Work History

By far, the most important part of your resume is your work history. This is the section that tells the hiring manager how easy you'll be to train and work with. There are really only two options here: either you've got it, or you don't.

Long Work History

If you already have experience in your field, or a related field, then this part will be easy. Make sure you go into plenty of detail about what you did, how you did it, and how your presence in your former company helped improve their overall big picture.

If you have years of experience at multiple places, you might want to choose a top five; maybe the most recent, or the positions in which you made the most difference to the company. Fill in the remaining years with highlights, and let the hiring manager focus on the areas you've carefully pointed him or her towards. The point is to spend a long interview talking to them, not watching them flip through a ten-page resume.

Short Work History

In general, it's better to highlight your relevant working experience, but if you don't have much work history to draw on yet, then focus on beefing up what experience you do have.

Your last job flipping burgers can easily become a chance to discuss your excellent teamwork skills.

Your time as a waiter taught you to multitask with the best of them.

Walking dogs or being a childcare provider is all about being dependable.

Being a dishwasher or a custodian gave you valuable skills, like implementing and following detailed procedural lists.

If your work history is lacking even these opportunities, then focus on any other activity you can. What kinds of things have you been doing with your life when you weren't physically in class?

Are you now or were you ever a part of any sports teams, clubs, or organizations? Typically, these positions, even if they were mostly social clubs, have some sort of physical, educational, or philanthropic purpose that you can draw on.

Volunteer positions are another area you can draw on for work related skills. If you tutor classmates, help out at the local soup kitchen, or clean up the park once a year, these are good ways to fill in a sparse resume.

If it is relevant to your job, you could also use time spent traveling to add detail. This mostly applies to traveling abroad, particularly in regions where the company has branches, or if in your travels, you became proficient at speaking another language.

The more detail you can go into about real-world experience implementing the core characteristics of a good employee (teamwork, accountability, and things of the sort), the better chance you'll have at moving on to the next step.

References

Most companies ask for references with your resume, and yes, they will call them.

References are a key way that hiring managers check on your skills, how easy you are to work with, and any potential problems that hiring you presents. It's important that your references are as reliable and professional as your resume itself.

Always use professional references rather than personal references. Your hiring manager cares about how you are to work with, what your qualifications in the field are, and how reliable you are as an employee. They probably don't care much about the fact that you are a great brother or an excellent addition to your church choir. The people that you choose to use as references should be former bosses, colleagues, professors, or other professional contacts that know you in relation to your work.

Official letters of reference can be useful if they come from someone who personally knows the hiring manager or currently works for the company you're applying for; but for the most part, a generic "To whom it may concern" letter is not the best way to give a reference. Hiring managers are more likely to call or email someone to get their current opinion of you, rather than trust a letter you've been carrying around for who knows how long.

You must ask your references before you give out their personal information in an interview. If they are caught off guard, they may make a less than favorable impression that does nothing for your chances. This is usually an easy case of asking.

Make it easy for them by having all their information filled in already, as much as you know, and give them a heads up about what types of jobs you'll be applying for, so they'll know how to talk about you. If they want, you could even provide them with some basic points to highlight about your work.

It's always polite to call them or email them when a company has asked for your reference list, so they'll be prepared.

I know what you're asking: what should I do if I don't have any good professional references? You might have to get creative with what you consider professional.

Have you volunteered with any organizations lately? Have you spent any time with service-oriented groups? Were you a part of any clubs or organizations in school? Do you know anyone through LinkedIn or social media, in the industry or a relevant one, that is willing to vouch for your knowledge based on the conversations you've had or your reputation?

As tempting as it may be to pad this section with personal references who will say only good things about you, it's more useful for the company, and thus for you, if you find people who can give an honest picture of you as a worker.

Communication Skills

Communication involves two parties: the communicator and the audience. Within a single conversation, you could play both roles multiple times. Having good communication skills, therefore, is about being a great speaker and a great listener.

Listening and Gathering Information

It's really very simple: listen to what people are saying.

Don't be distracted by thinking about what you plan to say next. Focus on what they are telling you, and if you need more time to formulate a response, it's never a bad idea to summarize or clarify what you just heard.

Say something like "I understand that teamwork is a really important part of your operations. That's great. At my last position…" These sorts of transition statements help you put your attention on the information at hand, and communicate loud and clear that you got the message.

Asking intelligent questions is an important part of being a good listener. It helps to make sure that you ask the right type of questions to get exactly the information you need, and to keep the manager talking.

Keep your questions open-ended, so that they require more than a "yes" or "no" answer. When you ask questions that require a full explanation, you open up a chance that you'll get more information that you didn't even know you lacked.

Don't interrupt when they are speaking, even if you think of something you'd like to ask. Let them finish, and then go back to the topic that caught your interest. Ask follow-up questions to any line of conversation that seems both relevant and interesting.

Speaking Like a Pro

When you're in the speaking position of a conversation, the main thing you need to consider is what is the main message that you want to convey.

Are you trying to inform someone of facts, trying to negotiate a salary, or trying to persuade a manager to hire you over another candidate? Each part of your interview will have a different goal.

Presenting facts in a clear manner that encourages questions and interaction is important during an interview. It shows a manager that you will be able to hold your own in a business meeting. It also keeps that all-important conversation going.

Tailoring your presentation for the audience makes you look like a professional. If you're speaking to a single manager, a more casual style of speech helps promote a feeling of friendliness. Speaking to a panel of managers might require a more professional mode that allows you to address everyone equally.

Criticism may be a part of your interview, especially if you're discussing why you left a former company. Both giving and receiving criticism in a positive manner is a critical part of speaking.

You need to be able to communicate remorse for past regressions in a confident way. Focus on the future and on how you plan to implement new behaviors, rather than putting the focus on past mistakes.

When giving criticism, use the technique called the "praise sandwich". Say one good thing and one bad thing, followed by another good thing. This ensures that both the first and final impression given by your words is a positive one.

Negotiation and persuasion can be hard to master without coming across as a car salesman. The key is backing up your points with hard, provable data, rather than empty opinions. Instead of saying that you're the best candidate for the job because you will work hard for the company, quote the results from your last job as proof that you're a great choice. When negotiating for a higher salary, quote comparable salaries from industries in the same city as proof that your request is on-par with the market average for your position.

Dress for Success

Finally, let's discuss how you look for an interview.

This may seem backwards, because for you, it's the first thing you will lay out and put on when getting ready for an interview. But this is the easiest area to change at the last minute, and doesn't require you to remember anything once you've got it on.

Uniform

For most of the companies you'll be interviewing with, the dressier side of business casual is appropriate for an interview. This doesn't mean breaking out a three-piece suit. A pair of slacks and a tucked-in shirt are usually fine. Depending on the culture of the company, jeans might be appropriate, but it's usually best to err on the side of just overdressed. Women might also choose to wear a skirt or dress, again, depending on the company.

The big don'ts for interview attire include:

- Never wear shorts to an interview.
- Never wear flip flops or sandals to an interview.
- Never wear an offensive shirt to an interview. (Anything that promotes something or has words on it)

An easy way to streamline this process, when you're doing a lot of interviews and filling applications is to create a standard outfit ensemble. Choose an outfit that fits within the right style for the company's culture, fits properly, and makes you feel confident in your appearance.

Grooming

Maintaining a neat, well-groomed appearance is a no-brainer. If you look like a slob, you won't convince any manager that you're a reliable person to handle and represent their business.

If it's been a while since you've ventured out into the business world, the basic things you need to pay attention to are:

- Fingernails need to be clean and short. If you're a woman, you should probably avoid painted nails until you know what the company policies are.
- Your breath needs to smell good and your teeth should be clean. A nice smile is part of a good first impression, and yellow teeth will ruin that in a heartbeat.
- Hair should be trimmed and clean. Facial hair doesn't have to be shaved off, but it should be neatly groomed.
- Makeup should be natural looking, unless you're specifically applying for an artistic position or a

position in the fashion industry.
- Your cologne or perfume shouldn't be overpowering. You don't want them to be able to smell you after you leave or before you get there.

Overall, how you present yourself is every bit as important as the skills you bring to the table. Knowing what to highlight about yourself helps you target and achieve your ideal job situation and makes interviewing easier if not a bit repetitive, since the process is pretty much: wash, rinse and repeat over and over again until you get a job offer.

PART TWO: THEM

Part One addressed the things you'll need to make yourself ready for an interview. In Part Two, we're going to talk about the process from the company's point of view and dive into the specific details of the hiring process and an interview.

Despite how it may seem when you meet some of your coworkers, companies don't just hire warm bodies. Employees are there to serve individual purposes, but also to help the company meet its overall goals. Understanding those goals will help you start to unlock the "whys" behind a company's hiring choices.

A business goal goes deeper than just the product or service they offer. You have to look at what benefit the product or service gives back to the organization. The company's mission statement, which can usually be found on their website, will usually give you a good idea of what their goals are.

Some companies, or even the majority of companies, exist to turn a profit. They believe their product or service is useful, but the profit is the ultimate goal. For these companies, employees that have great multitasking skills and strong communication abilities are highly valued.

Others are in place to fulfill a sense of duty to a cause or group. Companies in this area are more likely to hire employees that have strong work ethics and a lot of passion and energy to go around.

Still others are in place to further the progress in certain industries, where employees who possess analytical thinking skills and higher education degrees are valued.

Regardless of what their bottom line is, every company has needs that both do and don't directly relate to their immediate business. Even a one-man bike repair shop will eventually need a bookkeeper and someone to answer the phones. Support staff and teams that follow side projects are just as important to a company's progress.

We'll talk about how to discover what a company's goals and needs are later in Part Two. Understanding these two facets of business will help you target the proper companies to apply to, as well as help you get through the interview with all the right answers.

3. THE APPLICATION PROCESS

Understanding a specific company's application and hiring process is all about what I like to call Preparation H, where the H stands for Homework, and the homework is the relief medication that companies need from their prospective employees. Doing your research before you apply helps you tailor your approach every step of the way, which can only help your chances of getting hired.

Research

Before your first phone screen or initial talk with a company, you have to research the company, figure out what they do, or what industry or space they're in. Even if it's a surface level understanding. The reason for this is because they will ask you questions about their company and use that as a gauge to how you've prepared and they want to hear about your impression of their organization and more importantly if you've thought about how you fit in within their organization and culture.

A lot of the time, when I go to a company's website, I'm still confused as to what they do, either their website isn't laid out well, their mission statement is vague, or simply put their website has a lot of content but none of it means anything and is just an attempt to have something for the sake of having an online presence.

An unorganized website like this, with no clear mission statement, tells you that either they don't know what their core goal is or that they are just disorganized. So, when you talk to them, you'll have to be sure to ask the right questions to get more details into what they do, and what kind of skills they need from their employees.

When their site fails big time, I do another web search and try to get a clearer picture. That way, when the dreaded question of "Do you know what we do?" comes up, I can relate to the person on the other end with what my impression was of what they do, and get clarification without making myself look like I didn't do my research or give them harsh criticism about their poor online presence.

You should also have an idea of what they are planning to do in the future, especially if you are seeking a company with opportunities for long-term career moves. Look at what the major news articles are saying about the company.

If you can find this information, consider why they are hiring. Have they recently had a boom in the industry? Are they opening a new branch? Has there been a change in management or ownership of the company? Has the company recently gone public? All these things can be an indicator of why they might be looking to hire new employees now. Or do they have a high turnover rate? This could mean that there are internal issues to be wary of and might not be the best workplace due to some reason and from my experience – these issues usually stem from <u>incredibly poor</u> management.

Having all this information can help you decide whether you are truly interested in working for this particular company.

Other things that you will want to understand will be about the team dynamics, skill building opportunities, and workplace amenities, among other internal factors. However, the problem is that usually these things have to be asked across a team interview and requires observation of the company environment and the generational vibe of the workplace e.g. the average age range of the employees. It's impossible to get all of this information online, even glassdoor.com can only paint a small picture of only one team in a whole company or the reviews on a company may be non-existent, so you will have to do old fashion investigating.

Answering these questions will help you get the best understanding and feeling for a company and help you to tailor your interview questions and answers even more.

Sending an Application

Every company will have a different method they want you to follow for applying.

Some prefer that you fill out an online form and attach a resume. Others will draw your resume from a recruiter or aggregation site. You might simply be directed to email a resume to the hiring manager. If it's a very small company, you may just have to go to the location and apply in person.

When emailing an application, there are a few basic things to keep in mind. Don't just write "Dear Manager" or "Dear Sir". Do your research and find the name of the hiring manager. If there's no name listed, or you can't get their name after a cursory phone call, then even addressing your cover letter to the general manager is better than a generic greeting.

Make sure you spell their name correctly, even more so if they have a unique name. It will make you stand out from a long line of misspelled applications.

Cover letters can be a struggle, especially if you're used to hunting down leads on an aggregation site where companies come to you. Cover letters are still relevant for many companies out there, and yours needs to be just as clear and more concise than your resume.

The usual advice is to avoid starting all your sentences with "I" or "My", and to focus on how your skill set will benefit the company. You need to use language that is specific to your industry, and make sure that your intent is clearly communicated throughout the entire letter.

Keep your cover letter brief and to the point. The first paragraph should clearly state your intention to apply for a specific opening or position. You should communicate the highlights of your most recent work or education experience, and focus on the top qualities or skills that you have that would make you worth talking to further.

Conclude with a firm sign off that thanks them for their time, and make sure that all your contact information is clearly added.

Initial Phone Screen

A phone screen is often a precursor to an in-person interview, so consider it just as important to get right as the interview itself.

The biggest problem you'll run into with these screens in my experience is with two things, firstly, the higher the volume of phone screens that you do the more you will find yourself repeating the same things that you've said in previous phone screens, this is due to the person screening you asking the same questions as the other 10 people who came before had asked, this is unavoidable and is just part of the process. The second issue is if the person on the other end starts the screen demanding to know about you without introducing themselves. I mean would you go up to a stranger on the street and start grilling them right away without introducing themselves and warming you up a bit first? A true professional within the company will identify themselves first. In these cases, I immediately ask to know who I'm speaking to and what their role is, in a friendly tone of course. If they don't answer and try to power play, I hang up. It's better to cut your losses here than have to deal with an unprofessional employee or manager. Because I strongly believe that the key to a good working relationship is mutual respect between parties.

There are a few types of phone screens to be aware of, and many don't even involve a hiring manager. Knowing this information now keeps you from wasting time trying to impress someone who is simply collecting data, and has no say in the hiring process.

Recruiters

All they need to know is that **you can do the job**. There's no need to go into super intricate detail as you would in an interview, because they are just trying to build a database of workers who are interested and who have the skills that are required for the job. It's still important to be pleasant and make a decent impression because, as we discussed in Chapter 1, a good recruiter can be an important ally.

Recruiters Not Employed by Direct Company

These are independent data collectors whose only purpose is to grease the wheels during an interview. All you need to do is answer the questions in a straightforward manner so that they can pass the information on to the hiring manager.

A lot of the foreign recruiters will ask for your social security number and other sensitive information. Don't give them any sensitive information, because they aren't connected to the company at all and because this is still the screening stage and you haven't been made an offer yet so there's no reason for them to need this information.

Recruiters Within the Direct Company

Sometimes companies will hire dedicated people to sort and screen potential candidates for the roles that they are looking for, and it's also a good way to do an initial screening for an employee that will fit in with the company culture.

While this isn't the hiring manager who needs to know all the details of your previous work, you still want to come across as knowledgeable and likable here. Make sure that they can relate your work experience to what they are looking for, and that they leave the conversation with the impression that you'd be an asset and not a liability.

Hiring Manager

Over the phone, the hiring manager wants to hear briefly about your history, and they want to hear more specifically how your past relates to what they are looking for now. It's always good to ask them to clarify exactly what they need from this screening, so that you can pick and choose exactly which experiences would be more beneficial to share.

The manager also wants to make sure that you are pleasant enough, and can get along with their current team, so again, try to leave the manager with an overall feeling that you are easy to work with and more than competent.

Following Up

After applying, you get to play the waiting game. How soon the company will respond to an application largely depends on their size and current workload. If you are responding to a job posting, you're probably more likely to hear something quickly than if you sent a blind application.

Following up can be a tricky situation, because you want to keep your name in their mind without being written off as a pest. There are two factors when considering how to follow up: 'when', and 'how'.

When to Follow Up

Most industry professionals recommend following up after a week, which is plenty of time to allow for in-office discussions of your performance, and to let them cycle through and evaluate the other candidates, they had interviewed that week.

However, it's always a good idea to tailor your approach, just like every other part of the job hunt. If the company you've applied to is in the middle of a huge event, like a charity event or a major tour, you may want to wait until after to follow up. If the news is that they're hiring people left and right, you might want to follow up after only a few days. Again, research is your best friend.

How to Follow Up

For today's companies, following up by email is probably your best bet. It's likely how you applied, so you can reply to your original email to make it even easier for them to find your information. It's a no-pressure way to communicate that won't put anyone on the spot, and everyone appreciates that.

Your email should be short and sweet. State your intention to follow up, thank them for their time, and move on. Any more is not really necessary because all you want to know is if you are getting the job or not.

If the email you sent your application to was a generic company email rather than an email address with a person's name in the address, this may be a good situation to follow up with a phone call. The phone call serves the same purpose as the email, and should be in the same format.

Ask for the hiring manager by name, and then express your interest in following up with your application. Have all your information handy so they can easily look you up.

After a total of one – or possibly two – follow ups without an interview, it's time to move on. Any more than that, and your name gets on their radar for all the wrong reasons. Some professionals also recommend that your second follow up, if you choose to do that, should end with a sentence inviting them to keep your information on file, so they can contact you should another position open in the future.

Staying Organized

When you're filling out a few dozen applications, taking calls left and right, and trying to remember which week to follow up with which contact, it can get overwhelming fast.

One thing you can do is to keep everything on the same schedule: apply for a round of jobs on Day 1, send follow ups on Day 7, and then begin again the following week. Also, here are some ideas for keeping your networking events, follow-ups, and applications organized, plus a few sanity saving tips to make the whole process much smoother:

Get Friendly with a Calendar

Whether you use your phone, tablet, computer, or a physical calendar, you need something that allows you to label things with different tags or colors.

- Put your networking events in one color or label.
- Mark when you sent applications with a simple note for the company name.
- Mark dates for follow ups for the companies you applied to.
- Schedule coffee dates or lunch meetings with valuable contacts.
- Schedule your job hunt goals for each week, and review what you accomplished at the end of each week.

Spreadsheets are Your Friend

Spreadsheets will keep all your conflicting information in an easy-to-see system. You can keep track of companies, what their current job openings are, who your contacts within the company are, how and when you applied, how and when you followed up, and any other information you might want.

You can also use spreadsheets to help track contacts made at networking events or through social media. Use it like a searchable Rolodex of names, numbers, and email addresses, as well as personal notes to remind you of how you met, what topics you had in common, and any key words you want to remember when speaking to them.

Save Everything

Save your cover letter. Save your application answers. Save your interview answers. Keep all this information in documents that can be copied and pasted, reviewed, and printed later.

With a few tweaks to make it personal to the company and the hiring manager, a cover letter can be re-used, especially if you are applying in the same field. Save this in a Dropbox folder or on your Google Drive so that you can access it anywhere. That way when you're out running down leads, you can take advantage of any opportunity you come across with just a few quick changes.

Many, many applications require exactly the same information, and typing it all again and again wastes your time. If you're having a phone screening, you can keep this document open and simply read from it, rather than hunting down your resume and remembering all your information off the top of your head.

Saving your interview answers allows you to study and improve your answers for the tough questions. You can easily analyze where you can improve your answers, and it's also great for getting feedback from friends and colleagues.

Email Folders

Optimize your email to make it as easy to keep track of new messages as possible.

- Flag the names of recruiters or hiring managers that you have been working closely with, so their emails go right to the top.
- Keep responses to applications in a separate folder that you can review later, especially if the were negative responses that included feedback.
- Keep drafts ready with cover letters and attached resumes that only need a few updates to make them ready to send.

The application process might seem like a lot of technical tasks at first, but after filling out two or three dozen, you'll be able to race through these in no time flat.

4. INTERVIEWS

Getting that in-person interview is an exciting moment after you've been filling out applications for what seems like forever. Often, it feels like if you could just get that one chance to speak to someone in person, you'll be able to work your way out of the slush pile of resumes and into a job contract.

The call for an interview doesn't mean you're out of the woods just yet. I discussed in Chapter 2 about how to present yourself in an interview, and gave you a few basic tips to help you make a great first impression. Now let's look at the interview process in detail.

So the typical process entails that you will meet with various people for an allotted amount of time. Some companies will try to abuse your time and have you spend half a day (up to 4 hours) to a full day, just talking to person after person and repeating yourself over and over again for each person and then the whole thing can get derailed from messing up with one person.

So to prevent this abuse of time and save myself on time, I will tell the interview coordinator that I can't commit the whole time on one day and that I need it to be split into 2-3 sessions. This way if after the first session you hate everyone or it's not working out, then you don't have to return for the other sessions and you've just saved yourself a boat-load of time and energy.

At the interview, the hiring manager will be making assumptions about you based on how you present yourself and the answers you give to their questions. This isn't a bad thing; it's just how it works. It's your job to make sure that those assumptions are good ones.

From the moment you walk through the company's doors, you need to be directing any opinions of you from others in a positive direction. This means you have to impress more than just the manager. They'll probably ask their secretary if you were polite and on time, and they may even arrange to have potential co-workers meet you at the door to "escort" you, and then ask for their opinion later.

Be aware that every person you meet is a potential interviewer that day.

Be Prepared

Being prepared for your interview is always the first step. You'll need to be on time, with resume copies and a portfolio presentation ready to go.

The first thing you need to do is be promptly on time. Some managers won't appreciate if you are late and might hold it against you when considering you for the position against other candidates.

You also don't need to be hours early, though. That just makes it awkward because you will be sitting for an hour devaluing your image and conveying that your time is not valuable. Fifteen minutes early to check in, and filling out any paperwork, is more than enough.

There was one time when I had left early to go drive to an

interview site, and got to the general area where the office for an interview was located. At first, I couldn't figure out how to get to the building, and once I got into their office structure, I couldn't find the office number that I was looking for. The entire office structure was an immeasurable labyrinth, with offices buried inside with no clear map. I received a call from the in-house recruiter, who exploded at me because I was a minute late trying to figure out how to get to a place buried deeper than the Vatican's secrets. Needless to say, I never got to meet that hiring manager in person, and also that job opportunity was gone. The moral of the story is, don't pick up the phone if you are running late, and if you know ahead of time you will be running late then it's perfectly fine to call to let them know ahead of time. Also if you are unfamiliar with the area or the building that you will be heading to for the interview, be sure you leave enough time in case you get lost.

A more uplifting story came the time I got stuck in traffic to get to an interview. I finally arrived, met with the hiring director, and thanked him for waiting, noting that I didn't expect there to be so much traffic at this hour. The security guard looked at me and shook his head and was silently cracking up, and the director was cool as a cucumber and empathetic about it, which I ended up landing the job and had a decent working relation with him.

I have noticed that if you apologize, especially in American culture, it sometimes makes you come across as weak or indecisive. Instead, don't apologize; treat it as if they are doing you a favor, thank them for it, and then add a 'because' statement in order to garner some empathy.

Moving on, make sure to bring multiple copies of your resume with you to an interview. While most companies use a single hiring manager, you may be faced with more than one person during the interview. The manager might be accompanied by someone from HR, by their boss, by a panel of interviewers, or by a team leader. You want to make sure that anyone who needs to look at your resume has that option.

If your resume was submitted on your behalf by a recruiter, there's also a chance that they converted a document incorrectly, or printed it incorrectly, making your resume look less than stylish. Having your own carefully crafted and designed resume with you looks a lot more professional.

You should have your portfolio with you, but you should also be ready to present without it. They may also prefer to wait until a second interview to see a portfolio, so you might be discussing your work blindly on the first round. A picture may paint a thousand words, but you need to be able to communicate those words without the picture if necessary.

Answering Questions

The questions that you'll be asked during an interview are critical to get right. That doesn't mean that you must have the right answer for every question, but the way that you handle questions can give the manager the sense that you are a valuable employee.

For the most part, you'll get the regular questions asking about your last jobs, your education, and your other previous experience. Remember to go into detail, just like your resume. Emphasize anything you did that translates into the universal skills that all companies look for. One of the best ways to answer questions about your previous work is to follow the WAR method:

- **What happened,** and the
- **Action You Took,** and the
- **Results** You Achieved

It's an easy acronym to remember that gives you a handy template to follow. When they ask how you improved your last project, or what you brought to the table at your last job, go to WAR.

Tell them about a situation or task that was given to you. Explain the details of that project.

Then tell them what action you took, in a step-by-step format that shows your thought process.

And finally, talk about the results you achieved, preferably in measurable data rather than generic statements, or at least with industry specific language.

Every now and then, you may get a hiring manager who likes to ask off-the-wall questions that are designed to help them understand how you think. Just like the personality tests and career placement quizzes that you've probably taken before, these questions have little real use. But they'll ask them anyway, so you'll need to be ready for them.

You definitely want to answer truthfully, but there are ways to phrase your answers that allow you to communicate what they want to know. In general, they are trying to find out if you can think outside the box, solve problems, and if you can communicate your solutions well.

For example, if you're going into a position that requires a lot of multitasking, they may ask you something like "If you woke up to find 5,000 new emails in your inbox, and you only had time to answer 50, how would you decide which to answer?" They want to know that you won't just start from the top, but rather that you'll use the filter and search options to take care of pressing matters first.

Another good example for those who are going into marketing and advertising: A very popular question to get in these positions is "Describe the color green to a person who has been blind from birth". They want to know that you understand how to use key words that capture emotions and big ideas, which is an important part of creating advertisements for products.

Your best bet with answering these questions is either to be brutally honest and realistic, or to use ridiculously over-the-top answers to emphasize big ideas that are still grounded in reality.

Since you can never know exactly if or what wacky questions you'll be asked by hiring managers, the best preparation for this part of the interview is to keep in mind what your best skills are, what the job requires, and what the company's overall goal is, and try to always make your answer apply to one of these things. One good trick if you need time to consider your answer is to repeat the question back with a slight change. Here's a list of the most commonly asked interview questions, and how I would answer them myself:

Where do you see yourself in 5 years?

I see myself being a proactive leader, leading my own team towards success through mentoring, implementing better practices towards development, having things more streamlined and constantly pushing everyone to perform at the level that they were born to perform.

Why are you still doing this kind of work after being in the game for so long?

I'm the type of person who gets bored doing the same thing over and over again. Frankly, the reason why I've been in this game for so long, and still am in the game, is because it's always changing. What it is today is considerably different from what it was years ago, and this is always challenging me to adapt and to grow my skill set in order to still be relevant in this industry. That excites me to no end, and that's why I'm still doing this kind of work.

Why do you have a track record of short stints with companies?

I have a problem with mediocrity, and am always striving for the best. There are a few companies that I was only with for a short period of time, but I feel that I learned a lot in my time there, and have made a lasting impact at those companies through my contributions in terms of workflow and processes.

Why do you have large gaps in employment?

I have been spending my time in between working on different projects as an independent contractor, building single page apps for multiple clients. I have also spent a specific amount of time enrolled in a course or certificate program in order to build up my experience in (this specific subject).

Why are you currently looking to leave your current employer?

There are two ways to handle this question depending on the extent of your problems with your current employer. It's important to note that with either of these options, you should not come across as complaining about your employer. That communicates to the hiring manager that you would be willing to talk badly about this new company if your time there ever came to an end.

First, if there have been interpersonal problems at the current employer, you can freely state that the reason you are looking to leave your current employer is because the current workplace has become hostile with a co-worker or manager who is creating this negative environment, and that you had expected the current employer to have been more professional. Use that praise sandwich to couch this statement in generic positives, so you don't sound like a disgruntled employee with an axe to grind.

The other option you have, if you are just bored at the current employer and looking to move up the ladder, is to state that you feel that you've reached a stopping point in the progression of your career.

Explain what steps, in detail, that you have taken with your current supervisors to attempt to move up in the company, despite the lack of communication and any stalling in your learning and advancement within that company so far. If you feel that it's in your best interest to move on to a new opportunity, explain how you feel that the move will be beneficial to all the parties involved.

Why do you not have skills in (specific thing)?

Simply put, I have not had exposure in (specific thing) because I have been using this (other thing) instead. I have been curious about it, but haven't had the chance to use it yet.

This is also the perfect place to discuss any study that you've done on your own into the specific thing, or ask questions that show you are interested in learning more.

Being willing to learn, and easy to teach, is a big positive to focus on when you're talking about skills you don't have.

Why do you want to work for us?

This is a slight trick question. I had a friend tell me once that he was asked this question, and his reply to the hiring manager was that a guy told him to go to their offices and interview with their company. I had to face-palm because my palm was already close to my face and it was convenient.

The reason why this question is frequently asked is to determine that you have researched the company in question, and that you have tried to line up your personal career goals with what this company is moving towards or is currently doing.

So for example the way I would answer this question would be like so:

The reason I want to work for your company is because I have researched your company and have seen that (you have two roads to take here with either of the below sentences):

- Your company is working with specific innovations in this industry, and I would very much love to be part of that innovation, in ideation and working in the unknown.
- Your company is working with (technology A). I have recently finished a course in (technology A), or have a big passion for (technology A) thanks to (relevant experience). I would like to grow and build more things utilizing (technology A) and also bringing in my education or experience to the company.

What are you looking for in your next position?

I'm looking for a manager who is more hands-off in terms of macro management. I work best when I have a certain amount of freedom in order to execute my projects. I'm also looking for a team that is passionate in this trade, is constantly on the edge of the technology spectrum, and is open-minded about new trends and new technology.

What is your biggest weakness?

Weapons that slice. Guns. Axes. Maces. Delicious Sandwiches. Apple Products

I joke too much sometimes, and it can make people not take me seriously. But to be honest, sometimes the best way to answer this question is to use a humorous over-exaggeration of something that is work related, but phrased in a way that could be positive for the job. For instance, "Sometimes I get so caught up in my work that I lose track of time until I get it done."

Asking Questions

An interview is not just for the company. You're also interviewing them, to be sure that this will be a good fit for you. You don't want to come off like you didn't do any research, so when you're asking your questions, make sure you frame it in ways that communicate your knowledge.

For example, instead of asking "What is the company's main focus?" (You should have researched this already), say "Your mission statement told me that you focus on (particular area) here. What other areas of interest does the business operate in?"

Because you did a lot of research already in the "what" of the company, the big things you'll be asking are the why.

Why are you currently hiring? If they are recently opening a new facility or expanding their business, that indicates more chances to move up in the future. On the other hand, if they experience a high rate of turnover, you'll want to question why that is. There may be an underlying issue that prevents you from wanting the job.

Why do you follow this particular procedure, or use that particular model? The story behind the company's current policies could give you valuable insight on how they go about solving problems. You'll also get an idea of how the team thinks.

What projects are coming up for you in the future? Again, this lets you assess the potential for growth inside the company, and gives you a discussion topic to refer back to when the hiring manager asks you what you can bring to the company.

What kind of team would I be working with in this position? Will it be a small team, with just one other person, or a large department? That will also give you another factor to consider when determining if a company is right for you. If the interview is going well, the hiring manager could give you some insight on the people you'll be potentially working directly with.

What are the strengths and weaknesses you see in your current team? In other words, you're trying to find out if there's already a gap where you can step in and make yourself necessary. If the hiring manager tells you that the team has great ideas but lacks organization skills, that gives you the chance to highlight your organizational abilities as the interview goes on.

Ask them about the position you'll be filling. What is its place in the company's operations? Find out how the position fits with the company's long-term goals. Ask what kind of progress the company expects to see from you within the first month, six months, and year. All of these questions can help you establish a good idea of the potential job security and expectations.

Ask about your manager or team leader. What is their leadership style? How long have they been the manager, and how long have they been in the industry? You may want to ask what kinds of people perform the best under this manager's style of leadership. These questions are designed to help you understand what your daily routine and challenges will be like. Working well under your manager's style is a big part of having a successful job.

What is the most difficult season or month for this particular position? Some jobs may have a particularly busy or challenging time of the year when their work really picks up. For example, if you are applying to work in an accounting department, you are probably expecting tax time to be busy; but you may not know that the company has an annual audit every August. Knowing how often the department gets thrown into crisis mode can help you make a wise decision when choosing to accept or decline an offer.

Most hiring managers want to see employees who ask good questions, for two reasons.

The first is that asking intelligent questions indicates that you'll be willing to ask questions and clarify things as you're working. An employee who doesn't ask questions and instead blindly fumbles around a project, costs everyone time and money.

The second is that it shows that you have real interest in the company. Communicating with passion throughout the interview shows the manager that you've got energy and motivation to make yourself valuable.

Talking About Yourself

In any interview, you'll have to talk about yourself, and how your interests and passions relate to that field of work. The manager wants to know if you have the type of personality and values that line up with the majority of the other team members.

A lot of managers will also expect you to talk about your goals for the future, particularly with those questions like "where do you see yourself in five years?" Having firm, specific goals in mind, (remember my where do I see myself in five years response from chapter 4) is much better than a generic reply that tells them nothing about you.

Even if it sounds like an impossible goal, go ahead and dream big. Tell them that you see yourself as a team leader within a year if that's what you're working towards. They'll either be impressed by your work ethic, or their negative response will give you a key clue about the attitudes towards promotions in this company.

What do I typically talk about?

I begin by talking about my most recent two or three jobs. From the questions they ask as I'm speaking, it's easy to figure out what they want to hear more about. Once you find the topic that they can relate to, you can tailor the rest of your discussion to that.

I find something that I've done in the past that applies to the topic they responded to. Then we play the story game.

That's where they tell me a story, and I then I tell them a story. The more that you probe into the details of their stories, the better, because you'll walk out of the interview with a clear understanding of the type of person you are dealing with and what to potentially expect from them, and as an aside they'll feel appreciated because you took the time to listen to their stories.

Fixing a Bad Interview

If you are in the middle of an interview, and you can feel it going south quickly, it may not be just you. The hiring manager could be having a rough time, or this could be their first time interviewing candidates. Instead of giving up and letting the bad experience continue, here are some things to do to turn it around.

Rephrase Your Answers

If you think you gave a bad answer to a question, ask if you can rephrase it. Simply say, "Could I rephrase that answer? I think a better way to explain what I would do in that situation is…" and continue with your revised answer.

The key is to sound enthusiastic to give a great answer, rather than an answer that sounds like there was no consideration to it.

Face Big Problems Head On

If you are over qualified, under qualified, or have a red flag on your resume thanks to short job stints or a lack of education in the area, your first instinct might be to talk around those points. Focusing on the good rather than the bad may be the best solution.

But if the interview is going badly and you think you need to change the direction of the conversation, try facing those issues head on. Say frankly that you know you are over or under qualified, and then ask them if the two of you can discuss how that could be a problem. Offer several solutions for any points that they bring up during the discussion. Maybe you'd be willing to take some night courses to get caught up in an area you are under qualified for; maybe you'd be willing to offer training for no extra salary for a position you're over qualified for.

In any situation like this, you should always be prepared with some ways that you can still make this work.

Ask More Questions

If the hiring manager isn't following through with their end of the interview, or you notice that they seem tired or bored, then you need to ask more questions. Get them talking and keep them talking. You don't want to make them feel like they are being put on the spot, but just a few questions should be enough to get them interested in the conversation again.

Use Humor

Humor is sometimes a great trick to have up your sleeve because it gets people to interact with your words. They aren't just listening, they're also laughing. Self-deprecating humor can come across as needy or like you have low self-esteem, so instead, try to find a way to relate it to the job or situation at hand.

For example, if you are an editor and you mispronounce a common word in your nervousness, simply laugh at say "Wow, you'd never know my editing projects have won awards to hear me trip over that." Then correct yourself and move on. The shared chuckle is enough to smooth over the bump, and they'll probably never notice.

Ask for Feedback

If your interviews aren't resulting in jobs, asking for feedback from your latest interviewer can help you narrow down areas where you could improve. It could be something that you didn't even notice, like nervous body language, which is easy to fix. It could be that you need to update your resume to a more modern document, and fill it in with more volunteer positions or personal projects to fill in the work history gaps. It could be that you didn't answer the skills assessment questions to their satisfaction. It could be that they didn't like your handshake. But lots of times it can be hard to get honest feedback so it's important to press for more details on the feedback and then try to read between the lines of what they tell you.

After an Interview

There are two parts to the "after interview" stage.

Leaving the Interview

The first part is how you leave the interview. Thank them, of course, but then ask them when you can expect to hear back. If they don't give you a specific reply, ask when would be a good time for you to call back to follow up and get a business card or contact information. The goal for leaving the interview is to have a scheduled date in place for future contact. If you leave it open-ended, there's more chance that they won't even get back to you at all.

You may also want to consider what the last talking point you leave them with reveals about you. If you end the conversation discussing problems at your last job, since most people tend to start with the good and work their way to the bad, then the most recent impression they'll have of you will involve those potentially bad situations.

Instead, try to have a concluding question in your back pocket that you can pull out to impress right before you leave. So when they say "Do you have any more questions before we go?" you can reply with something like "Yes, one more. If you consider the people who have had this position before me, what was the key trait or skill that made the difference between those who were good at this job, and those who where great at it?"

If you can tell that the interviewer is pressed for time then it's perfectly fine to cut it short and tell them that you have no more questions currently and that you've had the majority of the questions you had in mind resolved and also, that you've hopefully painted a clear picture of your skillsets and abilities.

This tells the manager, right before you leave, that you're interested in being the absolute best you can be for the specific position.

Following Up

Following up with an interview is similar to following up with an application. You should usually do this over the phone, unless the manager specified that they prefer email. If you couldn't get them to commit to a date, call them back within a week.

If you can't find a good way to outright ask about the status of the position, start with a question. Tell them that you appreciated their time on the interview date, and that you had a follow up question regarding something they said during the interview. Ask it, get the answer, and then ask about the status.

It's an easy way to open the conversation, and getting them talking first will probably lead to a more honest answer about the position.

You'll probably go on more than one interview before you find that perfect job. Treat each one like a practice bout, and you'll quickly master all these mindsets and techniques that make you look and sound like the most qualified person they'll meet.

5. SKILLS ASSESSMENTS

Many companies, particularly in the computer science fields, require you to go through some skill assessment activities as part of an interview.

They may administer these as part of your individual interview, before or after the interview, or in a group with other potential applicants. There are many types of skill assessment tests, everything from a written exam to an oral presentation on the fly.

Here are the most common ones I've encountered.

Whiteboarding

The manager gives you a problem, and they want to see you physically work it out on a whiteboard. They'll want to know if you can communicate the steps of your work flow, and get to a solution quickly.

Whiteboarding lets them see your thought process in real-time, and it can be intimidating if you're more used to working on a computer with a keyboard. Personally I hate these, but it's a valuable way to prove that you can communicate your strategies and solutions towards problem solving.

Constructing Models

Provided that they don't want you to build a model of a theoretical system that isn't applicable to the real world, this can be a fairly painless process.

They'll give you a typical beginner's project, and time you as you build a decent model. If your industry is one that relies on producing software fixes, coding, or a physical model of a building or furniture design, then this should be a breeze.

Written Tests

For the most part, these are rare to find anymore. Most jobs rely on computerized tests if they are just collecting data. A written test could cover many things.

Just about anything relevant to the company is fair game. They may want to test your knowledge of standard operating procedures for the health care field if that is your industry. They may want to quiz your knowledge of stocks, or of basic computer programming short hand. If you're ready to work in your field, these types of tests should be easy.

A written test could also be a personality quiz or a behavioral assessment that helps the manager understand how you'll work with the team.

Some of the most popular personality tests include the Myer's Briggs, which is designed to help identify the core personality traits you might possess.

The Color Code test is a pretty similar questionnaire that simply divides people's personality traits into colors rather than letter indicators.

A personality test that is becoming very popular recently is the Sixteen Personality Factor Questionnaire (16PF Questionnaire). This one is on the rise because it's more about how your traits apply to practical situations, rather than simply assigning you generic traits.

Your written assessment could also be a practical skills exam like a typing test or mathematical exam. There are two different ways you could be given a written test:

Take Home Tests

This probably consists of an essay question or a mock report that they want you to prepare, or a mockup of a thing they want you to create, pretty much something that will take longer than the time they want to devote for a single interview. The upside to this kind of test is that if they like what you have submitted, you're likely to get a second round of interview or the primary round if the company starts off the bat with the test, or they may decide to make you an offer afterwards since you have made it this far in the process.

In-Person Tests

If they administer a written test during the interview, you're probably going to be timed. Test taking is a skill you may not have needed since high school, so if you think you'll encounter one of these, you can take some practice tests online before you go. When you get the call or email to arrange the interview, you can ask if they administer tests then, so you can schedule in plenty of time.

In the Field

If your industry is technical, like health care or computer repair, they may have you give a demonstration in the field.

Much like the model test, this will be easy as long as you

aren't asked to do something that is highly theoretical and rarely applies to the actual job. If you feel as though you've had a weak interview, this is an area where you can really shine.

How to Overcome Assessments

The only real way to get better at these assessments is through education. Take some courses, read some books, take on a practice project, or get a mentor to help you gain more knowledge in the areas that you feel that you are struggling with.

Taking a Course

Taking a course in the area you struggle with is the quickest way to understand and master new skills. You can easily get a handle on the basics with a course through a community college or center, or online. Official courses through accredited sources like a college can be added to your resume as official education that counts just as much as your degree.

On the downside, courses can be quite expensive, and you may have to jump through a few hoops to get in to the course. Having to pass some acceptance test to get in can be a pain, and the amount of time that some courses take to complete can mean that you have to put everything in your life on hold to accommodate the training. Also the scheduling can be inconvenient, as it may not take place in the timeframe that you need.

Reading Books

Reading books on the topic you need to brush up on is usually an easy and inexpensive way to get the information you need. If you don't want to buy them, you can request that your local library order a book. They don't require much time, and there's usually a wide range of information that can be found on a single topic. Finding books written by professionals or educators in the field ensures that you'll get accurate information.

However, some people just don't pick up concepts from text unless they can apply it on a project that requires real world problem solving. If you're the type of person who needs more hands-on learning, this might not be the best way to go about picking up new skills.

You also can't add "book reading" to your list of education on your resume, so it will be up to you to prove that you have a good handle on the topic during an actual interview.

Practice Projects

Designing and implementing a practice project in your field is a great way to gain experience and add a piece to add to your portfolio. You can learn to troubleshoot problems without access to company software and materials, which helps you build problem-solving skills specific to your industry.

If designing and creating your own project from scratch doesn't work for you, this is a good place to look for volunteer positions where you can get some practice in a real-world situation, and have something to add to your resume. Volunteer work that actually applies to your industry looks good on many levels.

Practice projects do take a lot of time and energy to put together. This can take away time from your main goal of finding a job, and it may also be expensive depending on your industry.

Mentors

Some concepts can be really hard to understand when spoken about in theory. If you're reading a book or taking a course that doesn't go into detail, you may require a mentor to break it down. Having someone with experience to quickly break down things that you don't understand is essential and having someone to be accountable to can be a great motivator to get off your butt and learn the subject matter at hand.

However, professional tutoring or mentorships can be pricey, and can also demand that you rearrange your schedule to fit into theirs. A free mentor might not have as much time to offer you, or may not be as reputable within the field, and can be really hard to find.

When faced with skills that you don't have a mastery over, taking the initiative yourself to improve can make all the difference in your next interview. It can give you a story that you can tell, about the problem you faced and the steps that you took to overcome it.

PART THREE: BRINGING IT ALL TOGETHER

The final part of this book brings everything together.

In Part One, we talked about your needs, and how you present yourself to be the best candidate.

In Part Two, we talked about the company's goals and how their interview process will work.

Now let's discuss how to make the relationship between you and your potential company beneficial for both of you.

A company is, in its own way, like a village. You have your home, which is where your office or desk is. You have your neighbors, with all the intricate personal politics that they can bring. There is a unique micro-culture within the company that dictates the general atmosphere and direction of the teams.

When you are considering accepting a job with a company, you should be thinking of that job in terms of how you will fit in with this new village.

Although you do have a chance to build on your reputation the longer you're with a company, those first impressions are still important. So before you even get a job offer, you may want to consider what your role will be within this new community.

This is where asking questions of the hiring manager in the interview can come in handy. It's just another type of research so you can be prepared for the next step.

If you do get a chance to tour the building, or walk by several desks before you go into the interview, try to notice anything you can about the space. What is on the walls? Are the desks personally decorated? Is the working space shared, and are people crammed together in small cubicles? This will tell you a lot about the daily atmosphere of the company.

Fitting in within the work place is about more than just being liked. Ultimately, it's about fulfilling needs on both ends. If you know there is a place where the team could be stronger, then you need to be preparing yourself to fill that gap. It's there for a reason.

Likewise, you need to consider how the company can fulfill your needs. We talked about those in Chapter 1.

If you need to live in a certain area, will the company keep you there? Is it more beneficial for them to send you to a different branch, and if so, how will you come to a compromise that suits you both?

Do your values give you a preference to work in a company that promotes and practices eco-friendly manufacturing? If the company you are applying to doesn't already do this, is there a way you can help implement some of those ideas?

Compromise is key to making sure that everyone gets what they need. This is what being in a relationship is all about.

In this section, we'll cover what to do when you get that job offer, how to negotiate for the salary and benefits you want, as well as how to record and use your results from getting this job to help you smooth out the process next time.

Finally, we'll look at some of the most common obstacles that prevent an individual and a company from making a good match.

6. CALIBRATION

As you go through the application, interview, and negotiation process, you're going to find a lot of things that could have gone differently, or better. Some of those things can be smoothed over with practice, but for others, you may need to make some effort to improve your presentation for the next go around.

Calibration is the act of fine-tuning an instrument or a process. When you need to calibrate your ability to apply and interview for a position, the first thing you need to do is to collect data. You need to know what you did wrong, where you went wrong, and how often you made mistakes in order to fix them.

People are creatures of habit, and we subconsciously rely on triggers for much of our behavior. As you start reviewing your previous applications, you might notice that you have a habit of saying "um" every time you are asked a question. Or you might notice a pattern where, you apply for a bunch of jobs online, but the cover letters that you submitted weren't targeted for those specific companies, which might have cost you the chance to interview.

If you can identify the triggers that cause your mistakes, like a question you weren't prepared for, or fatigue after a long day, you can work on recognizing them in the future, and improving your reaction.

So how do you go about gathering the data you need to learn these things? Looking back over your applications and resume is easy, but what about your interviews?

Recording

Recording your interviews gives you a way to review the way you sound, how your answers come across, and to fix any nervous speech tics like saying "um" during pauses, or clearing your throat when you are nervous. Also you can bring your own laptop and leave it recording yourself while the screen is showing a screensaver or the recording screen is minimized so it won't appear odd or out of place to the people interviewing you.

Write It Down

The easiest way to record your interviews is to write down your thoughts after you're done.

After each phone screening and in-person interview, jot down what went well, and what didn't. Try to list the questions that threw you for a loop, and brainstorm the answers that you would have given if you had time to prepare. Add any ideas you have about what you should do next time to fix the issues encountered.

Not only is this easy, it also gives you the chance to reflect on the experience immediately.

Recording Phone Calls

Taking an audio recording of your phone calls can be a tricky legal situation.

Recording other people's words isn't always legal, especially if they don't know they are being recorded. This is why you'll often hear a disclaimer when you call customer service that informs you that they may record your conversation for quality control purposes; staying on the line is giving your permission for them to do this.

There are eleven states that require both parties to consent to recording: California, Connecticut, Florida, Hawaii, Illinois, Maryland, Massachusetts, Montana, New Hampshire, Pennsylvania and Washington. If you live in one of these states, you have to inform the hiring manager or recruiter that you will be recording their words, and give them the opportunity to refuse.

Another thing you could do is simply record your own side of the conversation.

You won't get the complete context for reviewing later, or their questions, but if you combine this method with writing down what they said, you'll have an easy and legal record. Hearing yourself is important for learning how to speak more confidently, so this is a great choice.

If you can record the entire conversation, here are some methods and tools you can use:

- Use a basic tape recorder while your phone is on speaker.
- Use Google Voice. This app only works if the interviewer calls you, but it will email you a recording of your interview once you hang up.
- Use a telephone-recording device like the Olympus TP-8. This is an inexpensive device that plugs into any recorder. Then the earpiece listens to the conversation with you, recording what you hear, and picks up what you say.
- Phone apps like Call Recorder and Call Log Pro on

your cell phone can record phone conversations and send the recording straight to your Dropbox account.

If your interview takes place over Skype, you'll still have to follow the same laws about recording. Once you've made sure that it's legal to do so, here are some tools for recording a video interview:

- There is a lot of software that you can use to record a Skype video. Some have to be purchased and others are free. Software like Call Recorder for Skype, MP3 Skype Recorder, Tapur, Xsplit, iRecorder, and Call Trunk for Skype are easy to use, and you won't have to do anything other than press record.
- If all you need is the audio, you can use free software like Audacity to record your conversation. Just pull up a new Audacity project and record while you are speaking. You need to make sure that the interviewer is speaking through the speakers, not through your headphones. You can also do this with the built-in Sound Recorder or Media Player app on a PC.

Recording the skills assessment tests that you were given gives you a chance to study the types of questions that you'll find on these tests in the future. You probably won't run into exactly the same questions, but you can use it as a practice exam to learn how to take them as much as what material they cover.

- If the test is administered on your own computer, as a take home exam, you can easily save the file or take a screen capture of the exam.
- If it's a paper exam, or a test on a company console,

you could take a picture of the test with your cell phone. Apps like Google Goggles and Text Grabber will turn a picture into a document that you can use and edit.

After You Record

Once you have the material recorded, now you need to use it to study and tweak your behavior. Basic study techniques from your time in school or work training programs apply just the same.

Listen to the recording from start to finish. Try to hear yourself as a stranger would. Think about the way you sound and the words you use. Do you sound like a confident, competent person? If you were looking for a new employee, would you hire yourself?

I know personally for me, I've had times where I was watching or listening to playback of an interview and I was cringing at the way I had responded to specific questions and that event had forced me to fix my response for the next time and never to fumble on those things again. There were also times when I would see how my expression and tonality changed when I was getting irritated and it helped me to fine-tune those reactions and change what I do when those situations arose again.

Here are some things to write down as you listen:

- Areas where you didn't impress yourself, or where you didn't sound as confident as you should have
- If you think of a better way to phrase an answer that you gave
- If you notice any patterns of behavior that could be eliminated or changed

- If you think of answers to questions that you couldn't answer then
- Questions that caught you off guard
- Ideas for leaving the interview on a more positive note

Outsourcing Feedback

Once you've noted everything that you can, you may want to ask a friend or family member to help you out.

They can review your interviews to give you feedback as a third party. Ask them to consider you as a potential employee for their job, and get their impression of you as an applicant. Have them take a look at your resume as well.

If you really want to improve, you can also hire someone to review your resume to make sure it communicates the correct things. Some bigger named recruiting agencies may offer this service as part of their onboarding for potential candidates they want to represent, or they may know someone who does. There are a number of things that a resume should communicate that you can ask them to look for.

Your resume should highlight your strengths and relevant experiences that will highlight the areas that you want to work towards and also with what companies in general are looking for in that current point in time; because what companies are looking for today is going to be completely different than what they were looking for 18 months ago. Some industries are faster paced than others so your requirements may vary.

Lastly, It should be formatted in an aesthetic way and get the point across about who you are and what you bring to the table. So, the quicker you can overcome the issues that you identify in your feedback and evaluations, the quicker you can calibrate your skills and style and make the next interview even better.

Now What?

So now that you know what's wrong, how do you fix it?

Speaking

If your problem is largely with speaking and answering questions that you weren't prepared for, practice is the best way to improve in this area.

Practicing presentations and interviews in the mirror, or with someone else, helps smooth out those bad behaviors, and also gives you the chance to practice your answers in a no-pressure environment.

If you're having a lot of trouble with speaking in front of strangers, you might want to consider looking for an improvisational class or a find a Toastmaster's organization nearby. You can get good tips from the professionals there, and immediate feedback that will help you identify problems you may not have even known you had. The more time you can spend speaking professionally off the top of your head, the easier it gets long term.

Assessments

Improving your test taking ability is more about learning some strategic steps for the next time you're faced with an exam.

If you can, look for the easy questions first, and get those out of the way. They help build confidence so you can move on to the harder questions with a feeling of accomplishment.

If you can, scan the exam for the key ideas or topics that you notice popping up, and jot down a few notes that come to mind before you begin. That helps get your thoughts in order before you have to begin writing official answers.

If it's a multiple choice question that you aren't sure of, eliminate the most obviously incorrect options, and then go with your gut between the other options.

One of the biggest mistakes reported by test givers across all ages and situations is changing an answer that you felt was correct the first time. Unless you absolutely know that your first answer was wrong after more thought, leave it be.

If there is time, review your exam when you finish instead of turning it in right away.

With these tips, you can analyze and improve on your past performance to make your next interview much better.

7. OBSTACLES

When it comes to making a good connection between yourself and a company, there are some obstacles that seem out of your control at first.

These things, which can't be anticipated, can still unfortunately have a major effect on your chances of being hired. You're going to have to learn how to deal with these unexpected speed bumps in order to keep moving towards your ultimate goal.

People Problems

When working with other people, you always have to deal with certain personality types that clash with your own. When you're hunting for a job, you might feel like you have to be nice to everyone you meet, but remember that you're looking for a good fit for you too.

When you've been constantly making and taking calls from recruiters and doing phone interviews, it can take its toll on you. Everyone needs to know the same information you've just repeated ten other times, and you end up sounding like a broken record to yourself. Eventually, you become more concise with your words, leaving out details that would have been excellent to provide to the last person on the list. (If I could record myself and just play it back during phone screen and for in-person interviews, or even have a soundboard with common phrases and stories, it would save me lots of energy on talking and money on hot green tea boiled to a scorching 205 degrees from Starbucks)

The important thing to keep in mind is that the detail you go into should be less the farther you are from a hiring manager.

Save the energy for the big guys, and give the recruiters and middlemen only what they need to move you up the list. You need to treat every hiring manager like they are your first call that day. Bring all your energy and enthusiasm there.

The bottom line is that when you interview with people who are not the hiring manager, they are just doing their job.

Try not to take it personally when you have to go through the process over and over. Their screening strategies are there to ensure that you both fit well. Even as you keep your energy saved for the hiring manager, try to be pleasant in these situations. You never know who is making notes that the hiring manager will refer to.

The worst thing you could do is come off as insubordinate, as someone who refuses to do things. If you become passive aggressive and start off on the verbal offensive, you'll only earn the ire of those who report directly to the people you hope to work for.

You've got to stay as cool as a cucumber. It doesn't mean treat everyone like they're your new best friends. It means don't lose your composure, and stay focused on the end goal: landing that job.

Jealously is something that you may have to deal with, particularly if you have specialized niche skills in a competitive industry like software engineering.

It's normal for people to become envious of a potential hire who is getting a lot of attention and special treatment. It's important that you focus on your own game, meaning that you should focus attention to your own strategies and stick to them. If your strategy is to ask a lot of questions, then don't worry about looking like you're demanding attention. Ask your questions.

The thing to remember is that jealousy is usually a symptom of fear or nervousness. A new hire indicates that there are changes coming. Someone's job may be in danger. You are one more person that they have to compete with for raises and promotions.

Yes, you want to try to make yourself a friend and an ally, but at the end of the day, your career goals are more important to your life than their insecurities.

Testing Problems

Sometimes those skill assessments can really come back to bite you.

I've been in situations where I thought I had it in the bag. I did extremely well with all the phone interviews, and I sold the manager and the company big chiefs on my abilities. Everything was looking great, and then it happened: Some guy asked a few obscure technical questions that had no practical applications for the job. In some cases, they had nothing to do with the job at all.

When my answers weren't satisfactory, he reported to his manager, and that led to them passing me over for another candidate. I've had this happen a few times in the past and while it's always irritating, it's impossible to predict.

What you can do is find out if they are going to test you, and ask what topics they cover in their assessments. If they object to giving you at last general topics, or try to brush it off as being easy, then insist that you are serious about getting the job, and that you prefer to be prepared. Let them know that you're not willing to leave things to chance.

This shows them that you'll be a studious employee, and gives you the chance to review the topics covered before the interview. That doesn't mean that they won't surprise you; in fact, they may go out of their way to surprise you because you asked. But at least you'll be confident in what you do know they plan to ask, and that confidence will help you bluff your way through non-related questions.

Culture and Fitting In

Anytime a company tries to force-feed me a list of its values, typically it's pretty meaningless.

How are you supposed to get a good feel for the environment you'll be potentially working in from a written list of someone else's goals and values? You need to know what the culture is actually like every day, which usually has nothing to do with a list of words.

A better gauge for company culture is to look around the office at the demographics. Look at the age and style of the people there. Are they young and casual? Young and formal? Middle aged and formal? What kind of diversity do you see in the group?

Also, you need to look at the environment. Is it a cubicle set up or is it more open space with no walls? Pay attention to the seating style.

The most intense version of this that I've seen was a

manager who sat behind his team, where he could see everything they were doing at a glance. That's not comfortable at all. I wouldn't want to be on edge all the time working in this style of seating.

Recruiters

I've had the displeasure to have to talk to a few recruiters who took their jobs either too seriously, or not seriously enough.

The biggest distinction that you want to make is whether this recruiter is first party or third party.

If the recruiter is an in-house employee, meaning that they work directly and solely for the hiring company, then you will have to treat the conversations with this person a bit more seriously. They could and probably do have some sway with the hiring manager. They will want to be able to paint a picture about who you are, your work history, and why you're currently on the market.

Now, if your recruiter is a third party, they will be looking for the same thing. However, you do not need to go into full details with them. The most contact they probably have with any given hiring manager is sending a batch of resumes once a month. With these recruiters, regardless of how seriously they take themselves, you can be shorter with your answers. Hold off on any long stories until they can get you an actual interview with the hiring manager.

Other Obstacles

Things like traffic, weather, and other freak accidents that you simply can't control will always be present. The world seems to have a knack for getting in the way when you're going after your goals.

The only way to combat this is to be prepared. Leave early, pack extra, and do your best to power through anything that comes up.

Staying focused on your goals when things are going wrong can be disheartening. There are a few things that you can do when it starts to feel like nothing can go right.

- **Remind yourself what your goals are.** Sit down and write out your goals for your career. Your 1-year, 3-year, and ultimate plan should be specific, with measurable steps that start small and work up to bigger and better goals.
- **Remember the times that things went well.** Think about the last time that you had a positive interview, or the last time you felt great about the results of an assessment. Even if you didn't get those jobs, there is a huge list of reasons why they could have chosen someone else. It doesn't negate the fact that you did a great job in that situation. Draw confidence from your successful performances.
- **Talk to a trusted friend or family member.** Sometimes a little outside perspective can help you realize that things aren't as bad as they seem. You can get caught up in chasing the goals, and experience a phenomenon known as tunnel vision. Everything else disappears except the goal, and the longer it takes to get to the goal, the less you see. Having someone point out the places where you've missed positive experiences and opportunities can help you remember that you're on the right track.
- **Imagine yourself achieving your goal.** It's a mind trick that a lot of the most successful business

people rely on. Close your eyes and consider what your life will look like when you have the job you want. Feel the pride you'll experience when you successfully negotiate your salary. Think about what your next goal will be after you reach this one. Visualization has been shown to help motivate you to keep going.

• **Find your Big Why.** Yes, you know what your goal is, and you know how you plan to achieve it. But why is it your goal? This reason needs to be more specific than just "I want to be rich" or "I want to be successful and happy". Sit down and really think about why you want the lifestyle that your career goals are leading towards. Do you want to make a difference in the lives of others? Are your goals in place because they will allow you to pursue your passions? Knowing the underlying reason for your goals can help you keep going even when it gets tough.

• **Take a different approach.** If you're worn out by the constant stream of phone interviews and perusing job aggregation sites, maybe it's time to start looking at other avenues. Have you exhausted your contacts for leads? Have you considered getting involved with the industry's social media presence? Have you tried sending blind applications to your dream companies? Take a day or two to chase some new avenues, and then come back to the methods from this book with new energy.

• **Fake it.** If you're tired of putting in applications, and you can't muster up the energy to care about yet another interview, sometimes you just have to fake it. Plaster on the realest looking smile you can and pretend that you're excited to be there. Even if you're not, the effort it takes to pretend usually melts away and becomes genuine after a while.

- **Don't let outside negativity affect you.** Reading news that only bemoans the current job market, or listening to other unemployed people complain about their lack of success can affect your motivation. You've got to guard against outside negativity. Remember that their goals aren't yours, and make a commitment to yourself that you will work even harder to achieve everything you want. Surrounding yourself with positive, successful people helps keep you in a positive state of mind. It's the simple law of attraction, and it works.

- **Take care of yourself.** Your health can affect your mood more than you realize. Make sure that you're staying fit and healthy during your job hunt. It'll keep your energy up, and make your focus sharper.

- **Focus on the best parts of applying and interviewing.** Sometimes the brain procrastinates by focusing on the worst parts of an upcoming experience. That paralyses you, and makes you stressed out. When you realize those thoughts are creeping in, refocus your brain on the parts you know you'll ace. Rehearse your presentation and try to get excited about the event.

- **Ask for help.** Everyone needs help sometimes. If you can, ask the last manager who interviewed you for feedback. Reach out to your network and see if anyone has any new leads or advice they can give.

At the end of the day, you're just going to have to create a plan and attack it. After you've cycled through the process and met your desired quota for the day, there's nothing left to do. Make sure that your plan is specific, with steps that you can put into action immediately. Then gather yourself together and go do them.

Long-term consistent effort is what is going to lay the groundwork for overcoming future roadblocks and in having future successes.

8. GETTING THE OFFER

So, you've finally gotten through all the long days of sending out applications and attending interviews that didn't go anywhere. Congratulations, you've been offered a job.

If you did your research, and have found a company that fits you, you are almost at the home stretch towards landing a job.

Now what?

The job offer and the negotiation stage sets the tone for your entire working relationship. Before you jump to accept that job offer, there are a few things you should do first.

Get It in Writing

Always, always, always get the job offer in writing before you count on anything.

Don't respond to a verbal offer with a commitment until you've seen it in writing. The offer needs to use specific language that includes all the points that were discussed in your interview.

Make sure it mentions how many hours you're expected to work per week, how many weeks of vacation time you get and how those are accrued, how the benefits package works, how and how much you'll be paid, and any other relevant points that you have discussed.

You may also wish to request that the job offer show in detail what your job responsibilities are. Particularly if you're going into a large company, where cross-training is the norm, you'll want to know exactly what it is that your position is supposed to be focused on.

Ask More Questions

You have to ask more questions in order to make sure that anything that was unclear or not directly stated is in fact going to be followed through.

If you thought of more questions after your interview, or there were a few that never got answered during the interview, now is a great time to get them answered. Trust your gut here. If you would feel more secure about joining this team after you understand more about their operations, then that is what you need to do. A manager that isn't interested in answering questions from a potential employee probably isn't one you want to work with.

You might also want to ask about the company's rules and regulations before you sign an employee contract. You may discover a policy that changes your mind about your desire to work there. No one should expect you to sign a contract without knowing the rules by which you'd be bound afterwards.

If you haven't already, ask how employees are evaluated, and how evaluations can affect pay, or if they do at all.

If you need more time to consider the job offer after you've looked through the written offer and asked questions, the best way to do this is to give the manager a date. Thank them for the information, and tell them that you're excited about the opportunity. Then say "I will be in touch by Tuesday (whatever day you choose) with a firm reply." Obviously, if they've indicated that the job has a specific start date, your reply date needs to be before then.

Once a company has gone through the trouble of giving you a written offer, you do have the chance to take it home and sleep on it. It's very unlikely that they will renege on the offer now, and if they did, maybe you didn't want to be working with them in the first place.

Negotiate

Negotiating your new job can be an intimidating experience, but it's not a taboo to be avoided. It's a necessary process that makes sure that there's no misinterpretation and that all expectations are laid out in clear writing.

For many young job seekers who grew up during an economic down time, you've probably internalized a lot of misinformation about not ruining your chances for a job by accepting their offer without question.

This is wrong.

They would not have offered you the job if they didn't intend to hire you. That doesn't mean that you'll get exactly what you want, but it does mean that a simple question about wiggle room in the budget probably won't cause them to send you packing. It's much harder and more time consuming to re-interview a dozen more candidates than it is for them to have a talk with you about salary.

So when you go into a negotiation discussion, stay confident. Everyone here has agreed that you are the best candidate for the job.

Don't take the negotiation personal. The money they are paying you doesn't reflect on you as a person; it's about the service you offer the business. Your service is a product that you are selling to them, like selling a car.

If you were going to buy a used car, the first thing you would do is look up the going price for that make and model online, right? Then you'd offer the lowest amount you could, because you know that you're going to get talked up. You and the seller will go back and forth between your highest and their lowest until a compromise is reached.

This is exactly what you and your potential boss are doing. That's how bargaining works, and there's nothing personal about it.

Your Goal

When you were doing your research to discover the types of companies in your area, you should have gotten a good idea of the average salaries offered for positions like yours. It's going to be hard to convince any company to pay above the average for your position based on local data. (If your goals are way, way above that number, you might be in the wrong industry.)

Remember that your goal probably shouldn't be related to how much money you actually need to live on.

Yes, you need to ensure that you can pay your bills. But the best chance you have to get the salary you want is to rely on the data for comparable positions to give you your goal range. Even if you can live comfortably on less, don't undervalue the work that you're doing.

Go into the meeting with this data in mind, and know your goal, which should be near the area average. Never reveal the lowest number you could accept and still take the job. Once an employer hears that number, why would they come up at all? Start high and do what you can to stay there.

Their Benefit

Focus on the value that they will get from your services, rather than the need you have for a specific salary.

This is where that area data comes in handy. It's a rubric that shows how your skill set is valued in the relevant industry. An employer really doesn't care that you need a certain amount to pay your bills, but they do care that their business is productive and profitable. Refer back to ways in which you improved these areas in your last job if you have that experience.

Speaking of your old job, you don't have to (and probably shouldn't) answer the question, "What did you make at your last company?" Instead, redirect the conversation by replying with something like, "I'm interested in considering positions that pay around $95k a year. Is that a number we can come close to here?"

More than Salary

Negotiating a job offer is about more than just your salary.

If they simply do not have the budget to pay what you want, but you still want to work with the company, then consider how you can make up for the loss in pay with other benefits.

Are they willing to give you a one-time sign up bonus to help ease the transition between salaries? What about a relocation allowance to make it easier to move to the new area?

Are they willing to give you an extra week of paid vacation every year, or work with you to create a more flexible working schedule? Maybe they'll allow you to work from home one day a week, saving you money on your commute, if you agree to $250 less a month on your salary.

What about uniform or equipment requirements? Would they be willing to cover the costs of your yearly needs if you come down $1,000 per year?

Maybe they'd be willing to pay you a transportation allowance if you have a far commute, or have to drive to meet with clients in the area. Can you negotiate with them to cover a higher percentage of this cost?

This may also be a good time to bring up a severance package, especially if the company is currently being rearranged or expanded. If they won't budge on your pay now, they might be willing to commit to a more attractive severance pay.

What about an office? If the typical layout in the company is cubicles, can you settle for less pay in exchange for the privacy and less daily stress than an office provides?

Do they have a tuition reimbursement plan, and are they willing to increase the percentage of your student loan payments that they will cover?

If you have children, will they cover some or all of your daycare expenses? This can be a huge burden to the parents of young children, and having your employer cover this bill can make a smaller paycheck go much further.

If you have to use your own phone or tablet for work related activities, will they pay for the service? Or will they cover the cost of annual replacement devices?

Are they willing to cover the cost of your membership to an industry-specific organization? For example, new project managers probably want to get involved with the PMI, the educational organization that helps get you the continuing education you need to stay relevant. These memberships can be pricey.

What about share options? Is this a company that is owned by its employees, and if so, can you negotiate for more shares in exchange for less pay? If you're someone who is savvy to the stock market and the investing world, this could be an option you want to consider.

Any combination of these benefits with a salary negotiation can create a package that works for both of you.

Promotions and Raises

Yes, you can negotiate your raise schedule, to an extent. There may be a company policy in place that controls this, but nothing stops you from asking about it. You may be able to negotiate how often you receive evaluations and raises in exchange for taking a smaller paycheck up front.

If you want to negotiate a quicker evaluation and raise process than the company's standard six months or a year, then nailing down firm dates is better than generalizations. Get the manager to commit to "April 10", or whatever date works for your situation, as the day that you will receive your evaluation and applicable raise.

Likewise, a specific raise amount is better than a generic statement that you'll receive a "performance based raise". Ask them to commit to a "10% raise for every perfect evaluation", or something similar that uses exact language, so you'll all know what to expect when the time comes.

If you can arrange a situation where you'll be doubling your salary in just a few short years, it may be worth accepting the lowball offer.

Accepting

Once you've gotten through your negotiations, make sure that you have a revised job offer that reflects the changes that were made.

Go through this with a fine-toothed comb and be sure that it lists absolutely everything you spoke about. You want a document you can refer back to if anything were to ever be disputed. Get both the hiring manager and the general manager or owner to sign this document as well.

Remember, negotiations don't stop just because you've accepted the job.

After working there for six months or a year, you can come back to the table with a new negotiation offer. This time, you'll have data specific to their company that shows how valuable you are, and that can be a game changer when you need a higher salary.

If a company, their employees, and their workplace culture is a perfect fit for you, it might be worth considering waiting until this later point to insist on the higher salary. Especially if you were able to negotiate for other benefits, choosing a job that will fulfill your career goals and make you happy might become more important to you in the long run. If this job acts as a stepping-stone to a better position, then the years spent a little broke could be worth it.

Above all, don't be afraid to ask again during your time at the company when the time is right. Again, it's all about the value they place on the benefits you're providing. The cost of products goes up every day, including your services. The worst they can do is say no; if you're a good employee, they're highly unlikely to fire you for simply asking.

PART FOUR: Q & A

In this book, we've covered all the material you need for finding the job that leads to your career goals.

In Part One, we discussed how you go about finding a position that helps you meet your needs and goals, and how to get yourself ready for the application process.

In Part Two, we talked about how to focus on the right company, and how the interview and hiring process works.

In Part Three, we went over how to make your relationship with a company work for both of you, and how to overcome some of the most common obstacles you'll face.

I've given you my no-nonsense advice for tackling every step of the process, and have covered most of the problems you'll meet along the way. If you know what you're going after, and you follow the process relentlessly, you will succeed.

In this section, I'm going to answer some of the common questions that I've heard or had myself during the job-hunting process. A lot of this is summarizing information that you've already heard in the previous chapters, but is critical that you understand it and have it ingrained in your thoughts.

If you've already read the book and studied the information in each chapter, this section can be used as a handy quick reference guide to refresh your memory on the big topics that we've talked about.

Basics

Where do I look for job opportunities?

- Job opportunities are found in a variety of places. Look for them via:
- Job aggregation websites
- Going through recruiters
- Getting involved with your industry colleagues on social media
- Searching postings on company websites
- Hunting through your own network connections for leads

How long should my job search take?

Unfortunately, it takes as long as it takes.

The key idea to follow here is the Law of Spamming Until Something Sticks. Keep applying and interviewing until the offer comes. There's no magic answer, but persistence will get you there.

What should I focus on when I apply for a job?

There are a few basic things that you should focus on when you are applying for a job:

- Your resume should be free of errors and well designed.
- Your portfolio should be interesting and well

rounded.
- You should come across as confident and competent, but not cocky.
- You should be able to answer questions, give a presentation, and take any assessment tests without the aid of your resume or portfolio to refer back to.

How should I dress for an interview?

The biggest rule of thumb is to tailor your outfit to the company. If their employees wear suits, you need to wear a suit. For every other environment, business casual is fine. Be sure that you are neatly groomed.

How should I prepare for an interview?

Remember that the key is Preparation H, where the H stands for homework.

Do your homework. Read up on the company's mission statement, goals, and try to find any news articles that you can on their current and future projects. Try to get an understanding of why they are hiring before you go in.

Do's

Should I use job aggregation websites in my job hunt? Should I use more than one website?

Yes. Look at job postings across multiple websites, and upload your application or resume to as many secure websites as you can. The more chances someone will look at your resume in those early days, the better.

Should I also send my resume directly to companies, or only rely on recruiters and job postings?

Yes. Send your resume directly to the companies that you want to work for the most. Blind applications (applying when you don't know if a job is available) may at least lead to your resume being kept on file for the next opening.

What should I do after I apply?

Be proactive and follow up.

Email or call after a week and ask to speak to the hiring manger. If you haven't received a request for an interview after another week, send a second follow up thanking them for their time and asking them to keep you on file for future openings.

What should I do after an interview?

If you left an interview with no firm follow up date, send a thank you email communicating how eager you are to speak again. Then move on to the next opportunity until you hear back.

What should I do if I can't overcome a specific issue?

Read this book over and over and take notes. Seriously review the chapters in Part Three, where I discuss troubleshooting and improving your performance.

How should I choose which companies I should focus on?

Make sure that you know what your main goals are for your career. Your goals should be specifically written, not generic. You need to know exactly what kind of life you want to be living in the next 5 or 10 years. Make sure that your goal can be broken down into a plan with specific steps.

The companies you focus on should fall in line with your goals.

<u>When I get an interview, what should I ask to prepare?</u>

- Directions, to the building and the office that you need to report to
- The name and title of the person you'll be seeing
- Where you should park
- How long the interview is expected to take
- If there will be an assessment test, and what topics it will cover
- If there are any additional materials, other than your resume and portfolio, that the interviewer would like to see
- If they require a presentation

<u>Should I negotiate my salary and benefits? What if it's my first job offer in a long time?</u>

Yes, you should try to negotiate your salary and benefits if you want to.

If you've made it all the way through the interviews and call backs, it's unlikely that the company wants to spend more time than they have to interviewing more candidates.

Don'ts

<u>How much information should I give, and when should I give it?</u>

Don't give out your Social Security number, or any other sensitive data, to anyone until you've signed an actual offer letter.

In general, save the most detail about your history and experience for the hiring manager.

<u>What should I do if an initial screening isn't going well?</u>

Don't waste time on the phone if you feel that it's going nowhere.

The third-party recruiters and screeners that you'll speak to on the phone, they don't usually have any sway with the hiring manager. If you can already tell that you won't fit in based on this screening, it's okay to cut your losses and move on.

<u>How should I handle questions that I don't feel comfortable answering?</u>

The simple answer is, don't answer them. There are some questions that a potential employer isn't legally allowed to ask, like questions regarding your family.

If you have children, or intend to, they may find a reason to not hire you. Employees with young children do have more sick days on average than others. They aren't allowed to ask if you have children, but they may try to casually slip something into the conversation. They may comment on their own children, hoping you'll reciprocate with a story about your own.

Be on the lookout for behaviors like this so you don't answer something that you may prefer not to.

Should I go out of my way, or act in a way that isn't "me", to make the hiring manager like me?

Don't forget that this is a two-way street. You are interviewing the company as much as they are interviewing you. If this is going to work for both of you, you need to be able to work comfortably. They need to know who you are, and how you operate, to make the best decision for everyone.

Other

What should I do when I keep failing to make the deal after multiple interviews?

If you can't seem to nail down a job offer after a lot of interviews and calls, you need to start recording yourself in some way and review your performance. There is something that you can be doing better to present yourself as the right candidate. You should focus on collecting data, feedback in order to improve your weak areas for your next interview.

What should I do when the screening process is taking more time than my last three interviews combined?

Try to save your energy for the hiring manager.

Be polite and pleasant, but keep your answers short and on topic of the job in question until you get to the person who will actually be hiring you. It's the hiring manager that you need to wow with your detailed experience and passion for the industry, so make sure you're ready for them.

How can I find out from just a quick interview whether I would like a company or not?

Most of the time, you'll walk past some offices or cubicles on your way to the interview; if not, ask to be given a tour.

Then look for the types of people you see, and what kind of decor and layout you see around the offices. Those things will give you clues about the atmosphere.

Resources

This list is a compilation of current websites and other resources that can help you find, research, and apply for jobs. It's mostly specific to the United States, but not all.

I've tried to choose only the resources that are legitimately helpful, including sites that we've already talked about in this book.

Websites

There are many, many websites out there designed to help you find jobs. If you work in a very specific niche field, a quick search should turn up job aggregation sites, social media topics, relevant blogs or community sites from people in your specific industry.

Job Aggregation sites

- http://www.indeed.com
- http://www.dice.com
- http://www.monster.com
- http://www.simplyhired.com
- http://www.careerbuilder.com (has international listings)
- http://www.linkedin.com/job/ (has high quality leads)
- http://www.mediabistro.com (has leads for journalism, publishing, and marketing
- http://www.glassdoor.com (job aggregation and company reviews)

- http://www.usajobs.gov: (official government site for federal job listings)

Cost of Living Resources

- http://www.craigslist.org
- http://www.apartments.com
- http://www.trulia.com
- http://www.zillow.com

Salary Research

- http://www.payscale.com: A research site that helps you uncover data about the average pay rate of positions across the country
- http://www.salary.com: One of the oldest research sites that help you uncover data about what jobs pay what
- http://www.city-data.com: An extremely helpful website that has data about the job market in almost any area in the United States. Salary, growth, demographics, and other important data can be found here, as well as a forum where you can get first hand information about the culture of a city or company.

Blogs

- http://www.about.com/careers: Owned by the New York Times, and full of advice and articles to help you deal with problems and challenges that you'll face after you get the job
- https://www.themuse.com/advice: Has articles on career guidance and tips on things like negotiation and deciding a career path

- http://blog.penelopetrunk.com/: She discusses things like personal brand, negotiation advice and talks about deciding a career path

Podcasts

Podcasts are still a great way to get education and hear from some of the leading business minds in industry.

This is especially great if you're driving around job-hunting all day; you can listen in the car as you fight traffic. Listen while you work out or even while you cook dinner.

Search for podcasts specific to your industry, and you're sure to find a few.

- Career Tools (https://player.fm/series/career-tools): An award winning podcast that focuses on setting SMART goals to meet your career goals
- The Competitive Edge (https://player.fm/series/the-competitive-edge): A podcast that features regular guests from some of the top leadership positions in business. Successful entrepreneurs, authors, and industry leaders give you their secrets to making it big.
- Stanford eCorner Podcast (http://ecorner.stanford.edu/podcasts.html): An educational course in the form of a podcast, taught by Stanford business professors
- Accidental Creative (http://www.accidentalcreative.com/category/podcasts/ac/): A podcast that delivers weekly content discussing how to find creative fulfillment in your career, and how to meet your goals, featuring regular guests

Books

You may not have cracked open a business book since college, but that shouldn't stop you. The newest publications focus on the particular challenges faced by today's job seekers.

Again, a specific search on your own industry is sure to lead to books that apply to your situation.

- What Next? by Michael Price: Covers a wide range of topics that help millennials decide how to proceed with stalled or barely started careers.
- Manager 3.0 by Brad Karsh: An updated guide to management that covers how to make big decisions and affect change on the company culture.
- The Quarter Life Breakthrough by Adam Smiley Poswolsky: A book geared for people in their mid to late twenties who want to break out of entry level positions and start doing work they actually care about.

COMPANION WEBSITE

As an extra benefit to this book I have created a companion website which can be found at:

http://www.nononsenseapproachtojob.com

on this website you will find any book updates, news, community forums, be able to ask follow up questions and get even more information about anything related to landing a job. I have created this site in order to have a more interactive forum to be able to connect with anyone who has gotten any value from this book. So come check out the website and bring your questions and comments and help grow the community of other people looking for no-nonsense information on landing a job.

WORKS CITED

The following is a list of resources that were used in the research and development of the contents of this book.

Duhigg, Charles. The Power of Habit: Why We Do What We Do in Life and Business. New York: Random House, 2012. Print.

Sinek, Simon. Start with Why: How Great Leaders Inspire Everyone to Take Action. New York: Portfolio, 2009. Print.

Carnegie, Dale. How to Win Friends and Influence People. New York: Simon and Schuster, 1981. Print.

Ries, Eric. The Lean Startup: How Today's Entrepreneurs Use Continuous Innovation to Create Radically Successful Businesses. New York: Crown Business, 2011. Print.

Kaufman, Josh. The Personal MBA: Master the Art of Business. New York, NY: Portfolio/Penguin, 2012. Print.

Eker, T. Harv. Secrets of the Millionaire Mind: Mastering the Inner Game of Wealth. New York: HarperCollins, 2005.

Print.

Howes, Lewis. The School of Greatness: A Real-world Guide for Living Bigger, Loving Deeper, and Leaving a Legacy. Rodale, 2015. Print.
Forbes. Forbes Magazine. Web.

So many articles from Forbes magazine have been helpful during the research and development of this book, that including the magazine as a source is a must. Specific articles that provided direct information for this book include but are not limited to:

Wang, Nelson. "10 Things You Should Start Doing Today To Motivate Yourself For Success." Forbes. Forbes Magazine, 14 Aug. 2015. Web.

Muse. "Yes, Cover Letters Still Matter -- And Yes, There's A Way To Make Yours Stand Out." Forbes. Forbes Magazine, 1 Feb. 2016. Web.

Warrell, Margie. "Use It Or Lose It: The Science Behind Self-Confidence." Forbes. Forbes Magazine, 27 Feb. 2015. Web.

Patel, Neil. "Networking Guide For Beginner Entrepreneurs." Forbes. Forbes Magazine, 14 Sept. 2015. Web.

ABOUT THE AUTHOR

Dion Yang, born and raised in the heart of New York City and later moved to the San Francisco Bay Area in order to pursue more career opportunities. He currently works as a visual software engineer and is a strong advocate for better working processes and conditions. He has worked in the online technology industry for many companies from small, medium to large corporations.

Through his 16 years of professional experience he has seen a lot of typical and also unique situations and through trial and error has figured out what it takes to find and land a job that is suited towards specific individual needs. He has also mentored and coached friends and associates to help them land positions that were better suited towards their goals and personality.